A War Not Won

A tribute to the men of the Army Combat
Engineers who courageously served their
country during the unpopular Vietnam War

Ernest D. Peixotto

Lieutenant General U.S. Army Retired

*A personal tribute to the men of the 86th Combat
Engineer Battalion who courageously served their
country during the very unpopular Vietnam War.
I shall always admire and love them. They may not
have been the kind of heroes we read about, but they
were the stuff of which heroes are made.*

A War Not Won
A tribute to the men of the Army Combat Engineers who
courageously served their country during the unpopular Vietnam War
Copyright © 2018 by Ernest D. Peixotto

Library of Congress Control Number: 2018946831
ISBN-13: Paperback: 978-1-64151-908-3
         PDF: 978-1-64151-909-0
         ePub: 978-1-64151-910-6
         Kindle: 978-1-64151-911-3

Printed in the United States of America

LitFire
PUBLISHING

LitFire LLC
1-800-511-9787
www.litfirepublishing.com
order@litfirepublishing.com

CONTENTS

INTRODUCTION

Many years after I retired from the Army, I had time to reflect on my experiences during the Vietnam War and the men of the 86th Combat Engineer Battalion. Those engineers had performed brilliantly in combat under extremely adverse conditions.

Why have I written about my experiences? I believe that it is important to give my personal account about the battalion's engineer soldiers and what they did for their country during a very unpopular war. More than one hundred and fifty of the battalion's soldiers were killed or wounded as they did their duty to carry out their many dangerous missions in the Mekong Delta of South Vietnam.

My account is based on personal notes, letters to my wife, a very few official records that I have recovered, and many memories that had been dormant for more than fifty years. It is not possible for me to recall all the many details, but to the best of my ability this report tells the story as I saw it and as I remember it. There may be errors in fact, but they are not intentional. I apologize in advance if I have made errors in men's names and for the many omitted names. I wish that I had kept better records.

The combat engineers of the 86th were a special lot of soldiers-engineers. I often think about the accomplishments of those heroic men who served so magnificently. They did their job and did not complain. Their hometown newspapers noted their names only when they were on the casualty lists. Their country's reward for their sacrifice was an honorable discharge and an occasional Bronze Star or Army Commendation Medal. They courageously faced constant danger from enemy attacks as they performed their assigned duties. They cleared jungles, built roads and bridges through dangerous Viet Cong sanctuary areas. They built base camps and fire support bases for infantry and artillery units of the 9th Division. They lived through nightly enemy mortar and rocket attacks, only to push further into Viet Cong held territory the next day. They cleared mines and removed booby traps. They built airfields and bridges. They were combat engineers in the finest tradition of the Army Engineers. In most cases their heroism did not come from a single act but from the daily danger from the enemy while they carried out their missions. I shall always admire and love them. They may not have been the kind of heroes we read about, but they were the stuff of which heroes are made.

When I completed my assignment as the commander of the 86th Combat Engineer Battalion in July of 1969, I returned to the US and was troubled that most American citizens were not concerned with the plight of their soldiers in combat. So many Americans opposed the war that our political leaders were looking for a way to abandon the war. President Nixon was negotiating for a peace that, in my opinion, was an admission of defeat.

After more than a decade of our involvement in Vietnam, the United States decided to withdraw from Vietnam. Our political leaders developed the term *Vietnamization* which meant that we declared victory and turned the war over to the South Vietnamese. Eventually, the United States left it up to the South Vietnamese to carry on the fight. Many of us in Vietnam knew they could not win the war by themselves.

The first units withdrawn from Vietnam were the US 9th Infantry Division and the 86th Combat Engineer Battalion. Thus, soon after I left the battalion in the summer of 1969, my battalion received orders to withdraw from Vietnam.

About 2,700,000 Americans had served their country during that unpopular and undeclared war. More than 58,000 died, and more than 300,000 were wounded. Were the hardships, the dangerous work, the deaths, the wounds, the sickness, and loneliness borne needlessly? Most tragic are the thousands of men who paid with their lives and whose 58,148 names are etched on the Vietnam Memorial in Washington. Was it worth it? I do not intend to try to answer that question. Only time will tell. For those of us who played a small part in the drama, it is disheartening to dwell on the thought.

I can testify that the young men of the 86th served their country with great distinction. Stories about poor discipline, drugs etc. were popular with the media, the movies, and authors. Those situations may have occurred in some Army units, particularly after the United States decided to withdraw. However, I believe the media exaggerated those stories and did a great disservice to the many veterans of the Vietnam War. The media caused the public to believe that it was a normal situation in Vietnam. I believe that most of the soldiers were as patriotic and as courageous as any of their predecessors in the history of the United States Army. In some respects, it took more courage for them to fight in an unpopular war.

A BRIEF HISTORY OF VIETNAM

French colonialists had ruled over the Vietnamese populace in French Indo China since 1887; however, a Vietnamese nationalist movement, led by Ho Chi Minh, arose in the early twentieth century, and gained momentum during World War II while the Japanese swept away French Colonial rule and occupied Vietnam. After the Japanese withdrew from Vietnam in 1945, the Viet Minh, a coalition of Nationalists and Communists, developed a republic. The French tried to reassert their control, but that resulted in the French-Indochina War (1946 to 1954), which ended when the Viet Minh defeated the French Army at Dien Bien Phu on 8 May 1954. The French withdrew from Vietnam.

The Geneva Peace Treaty of 1954, signed after the French defeat, created two countries, North and South Vietnam. Ngo Dinh Diem proclaimed the Republic of South Vietnam and became its president. The US recognized and supported the new republic by sending an ambassador and financial support.

To enforce the treaty, three neutral countries, India, Poland, and Canada were responsible for enforcing the terms of the treaty, which was a charade. The Indian, Canadian, and Polish military personnel stationed in Vietnam were ineffective.

Soon after they signed the Treaty, North Vietnam's communist leaders in Hanoi authorized the communists in South Vietnam, the Viet Cong, to begin a low-level insurgency. North Vietnam was determined to reunify the entire country and set out to use the already well-established guerrillas in South Vietnam to destroy the new government. The communists were well organized and confident after they had defeated the powerful French Army.

President Diem, the new President of South Vietnam, reacted by ordering a brutal campaign to execute and imprison thousands of local Viet Cong cadres and supporters. However, the insurgency increased as the Viet Cong assassinated four hundred government officials in 1957. While the terrorists aimed their first attacks at local government officials, they broadened their attacks to include other symbols of authority, such as schoolteachers, health workers, and agricultural officials. According to one estimate, the insurgents assassinated twenty percent of South Vietnam's village chiefs by the end of 1958. The insurgency sought to destroy Diem's control in South Vietnam's rural villages and replace it with a shadow government.

In April 1958, President Eisenhower made a commitment to support South Vietnam as a separate National State and the US began to assign a handful of military advisors to help train and equip South Vietnam's new army. President Eisenhower did not agree to commit US combat troops.

In January 1959, just a few months before my first arrival in Vietnam, North Vietnam's Central Committee issued a secret resolution authorizing an "armed struggle." The resolution directed the communists in South Vietnam to begin large-scale operations against the South Vietnamese military. North Vietnam supported that operation by supplying troops and supplies in earnest and began transporting thousands of men and tons of weapons down the Ho Chi Minh Trail to reinforce the insurgency.

FIRST VIETNAM ASSIGNMENT 1959-1960

I received orders for my first assignment to Vietnam on 10 December 1958, while I was a captain on duty with the Atomic Energy Commission in Washington, D.C. The Department of the Army orders assigned me to the Military Assistance Advisory Group (MAAG) Vietnam to be an advisor to the South Vietnamese Army. Those orders came as a total surprise to me.

In 1958, Vietnam was not a household name. When I mentioned that I was on orders to Vietnam, many friends asked where it was. I knew little about that country, except that it was a troubled area with guerrilla warfare. I did not know that at the very time I received orders to Vietnam, North Vietnam's Central Committee issued a secret resolution authorizing an "armed struggle."

Then, just before Christmas, the personnel officer in MAAG headquarters in Vietnam contacted me to propose that I accept a two-year assignment because I was to be assigned as the Engineer Advisor at Vietnam's newly established Military Academy, which was near the city of Dalat in an isolated mountain region one-hundred and ninety miles northeast of Saigon.

A two-year assignment allowed my wife, our six-year-old daughter, and our four-year-old son to go with me to Vietnam. Military Assistance Advisory Group officers assured me that Dalat was a peaceful place and a safe place for my family to live. Since the families of the senior officers assigned to the MAAG headquarters lived in Saigon, and the Army officer I would be working with in Dalat had his family there, it seemed it would be safe for my family to be with me. My wife and I knew very little about Vietnam to make an informed decision, but after discussing the pros and cons of the unique opportunity, we decided to go as a family.

My prior Army experience did little to prepare me to be an advisor to Vietnamese Army officers. After graduating from the U.S. Military Academy in 1951, I served as a Tactical Officer at the Engineer Officers Candidate School at Fort Belvoir, Platoon Leader with the 370th Engineer Amphibious Support Regiment in Panama, Assistant Battalion S-3, and Company Commander with the 16th Armored Engineer Battalion at Fort Hood, Texas. From Texas, I went on to serve as Assistant to the Commander of the Vicksburg Engineer District in Mississippi and then the Army sent me for post-graduate study at the Massachusetts Institute of Technology in Boston where I majored in both Civil Engineering and Nuclear Physics. After graduating from the MIT, I served with the Atomic Energy Commission as a project manager for a nuclear power plant.

While I was semi-fluent in Spanish, I did not speak Vietnamese or French, nor did the Army give me the opportunity to learn either language before I left. Instead, the Army ordered me to attend the three-month Advanced Engineer Officers course of instructions at Fort Belvoir, Virginia before I left for Vietnam.

We arrived in Saigon in June 1959 at a time when the US was working to save the new Republic. MAAG Vietnam's mission was to equip, organize, and train a South Vietnamese army the way the US Army was trained to fight. However, our Army lacked experience, equipment, and training to fight a guerrilla war. That was our first of many strategic mistakes in Vietnam. The US was already headed down a difficult road.

We made a lot of mistakes in Vietnam and my purpose is not to analyze those mistakes. However, from time to time I will comment, with the benefit of hindsight. Many writers would have us believe that they knew all the answers to winning the war. They remind me of the "Monday morning quarterback."

Figure 1 South Vietnam

While I was in Saigon for orientation briefings, senior officers told me that the Viet Cong would not attack US advisors, because they feared retaliation from Washington. I received orders that I was not to carry a weapon. However, shortly after arriving in Dalat, on 8 July 1959, the Viet Cong attacked the MAAG's compound in Bien Hoa while several advisors were watching an evening movie. The Viet Cong killed Major

Dale Richard Buis, the senior officer, and Master Sergeant Chester M. "Charles" Ovand. They were the first official US casualties of the war. The attack and the death of Major Buis and Master Sergeant Ovand was small news in the US, but that attack at Bien Hoa was a clear warning that all US Army advisors were fair game for the Viet Cong.

I was one of two US officers assigned as advisors to the Superintendent of the Vietnamese Military Academy, General Le Van Kim. Major James Christy was the infantry advisor. Our job was to help General Kim develop a strong officer corps to lead their new Army. At the time, the school was a glorified Officer Candidate School, housed in an old Japanese prisoner of war camp.

Figure 2 Vietnam Military Academy Cadets on parade

As the Engineer Advisor, I had two missions. First, develop a four-year university-level academic curriculum. Second, plan for and construct a modern campus for the Academy. I was to create something from nothing based on my limited experience and with little outside help.

Based on frequent discussions with General Kim, I developed a curriculum based on information I obtained from the Academic Department at West Point; however, much of West Point's curriculum was not applicable because the Vietnamese cadets did not have an academic background equal to that of West Point cadets. Education for the Vietnamese had been very inadequate under the French colonist. West Point textbooks were useless because they were in English and there were a limited number of textbooks available in Vietnamese and French. After working several months, General Kim approved my recommendations. I

Figure 3 Construction of Cadet barracks

7

then traveled to Saigon to MAAG headquarters where I briefed several key members of the staff and then Major General James Lampert, the deputy commander. He approved the curriculum and gave me authority to start getting the academic material.

Planning for a new campus required that I make preliminary decisions about the type and size of the academic classrooms and the cadet barracks, the number of cadets to live in a barracks room, the size and kind of mess hall and a gymnasium, the type of laboratories, and many other fundamental factors. Once General Kim approved those many factors, I produced a plan for the location and design of the cadet barracks, academic buildings, gymnasium, mess hall, headquarters,

Figure 4 President Ngo Dinh Diem lays the cornerstone

and other supporting facilities. General Kim and the Chief of the Engineer Branch at MAAG headquarters approved the plans in October 1959.

Architect engineers in Saigon prepared cost estimates and the engineering plans. The first earthwork for the roads and facility area began in late 1959, and construction of the academic and barracks buildings began early in 1960 by a Vietnamese contractor.

Vietnamese construction techniques were quite different from that which we used in the U.S., but they had been building that way under the French for many years. While not up to our standards, the work met Vietnamese specifications. That was not the time or place to modernize construction standards in Vietnam.

The President of Vietnam, Ngo Dinh Diem, flew to Dalat in March 1960 to place the cornerstone for the academy in the company of General Kim, Lieutenant General Lionel G. McGarr, the MAAG commander, and several other senior U.S. and Vietnamese generals.

My first Vietnam assignment ended suddenly in the fall of 1960, because I contracted a severe case of amoebic hepatitis. The Medics in Saigon evacuated me to the hospital at Clark Air Force Base in the Philippines. Once the Air Force doctors learned the extent of my problem, they evacuated me to Walter Reed Hospital in Washington, aboard an Air Force air ambulance.

*****

After my departure from Vietnam, newly elected President Kennedy began increasing our involvement in Vietnam and the United States assumed more and more of the responsibility for fighting the war. After President Kennedy's assassination in Dallas, Texas, President Johnson, along with Defense Secretary McNamara, continued to escalate our involvement without any clear strategy to win the war. They believed that if South Vietnam fell to the communists all Southeast Asia would follow suit. In the meantime, the North Vietnamese continued to move thousands of soldiers and tons of supplies into South Vietnam using the Ho Chi Minh trail, which went through Laos and Cambodia. It was a political decision not to bring those two countries into the war by our bombing this supply route.

*****

Seven years later, I volunteered to return to Vietnam on 24 January 1968, seven days before the infamous TET offensive of 1968. During those years since I had left Vietnam, I served in two research and development assignments, one with the Chief of Engineers and the other on the Army Staff in the Pentagon. Next, I attended the Command and General Staff College, and then was the Area Engineer in northeastern Iran supervising the construction of a large permanent jet airbase. When I decided to volunteer to return to Vietnam, I was the Special Assistant to the Chief of Engineers in Washington.

HISTORY OF THE 86ᵀᴴ IN VIETNAM

The 86ᵗʰ Engineer Battalion (Combat) (Army) served in Vietnam for about three years. When it arrived in Vietnam on 22 October 1966, the battalion was stationed at Phu Loi and assigned to the 79ᵗʰ Engineer Group in the 18ᵗʰ Engineer Brigade. Lieutenant Colonel Colin M. Carter commanded the battalion. During March and April of 1967, the battalion moved from Phu Loi to Camp Martin Cox at Bear Cat and assigned to the 34th Engineer Group of the 20th Engineer Brigade. At that time, Lieutenant Colonel James F. Miley, commanded the battalion.

On 22 September 1967 Lieutenant Colonel Clyde A. Selleck, Jr. assumed command of the battalion. On 2 August 1968, Lieutenant Colonel Selleck turned over the command to me, Lieutenant Colonel Ernest D. Peixotto, during a ceremony at Bear Cat. On 15 August 1968, the battalion moved into the Mekong Delta at Camp Viking, just to the west of My Tho. When I left the battalion in July 1969, preparations were underway to withdraw the battalion back to the US and deactivate it along with the 9th Infantry Division. I turned the command of the 86th over to Major Walter C. Bell. He managed the last few days of the battalion. The Vietnam War was over for the 86th. The United States had decided to *Vietnamize* the war and turn the fighting over to the South Vietnamese. The departure of the 9th Division and the 86th Engineer Battalion (Combat) left a void in the Mekong Delta; we knew that the Viet Cong would soon be back in control.

During its three years in Vietnam, the 86th Combat Engineer Battalion supported four US Divisions and three Vietnamese Army Divisions as well as many smaller units in both Armies. Specifically, it supported the 1st, 9th, 1st Air Mobile, and 101st Airborne (US) Divisions. The 11th Armored Cavalry Regiment and the 199th Light Infantry Brigade. It also supported the 7th, 9th and the 18th ARVN Divisions. The battalion operated in many areas of Vietnam; the II, III and IV Corps Tactical Zones.

The battalion took part in the following major operations: Enterprise, Paddington, Akron, Emporia I & II, Uniontown, Coronado II, Emporia III, That Man Le, Emporia IV, Richmond, Riley, Long Haul, Santa Fe, Manchester, Rooster, Plantation, Mallard I & II, Gainesville, Paul Bunyan, Peoples Road, Speedy Express and Enterprise. The battalion took part in over twenty major combat operations. In addition to those major operations the battalion was active in many other operations that did not enjoy the visibility of a major campaign.

Since I have no firsthand knowledge of the heroic efforts of the battalion before I assumed command, my story covers the period from August 1968 to July 1969.

ARRIVAL IN VIETNAM

Like every soldier that goes off to war, the hardest part was saying goodbye to my family. We said our farewells at Dulles International Airport on 28 July 1968 as I boarded a Boeing 707 going to Seattle. That was an emotionally distressing time. I loved my family very much and did not look forward to a long separation. The possibility that I might not return was always there, but both Libby and I have a strong Christian faith and we knew that our fate was in God's hands. We had learned to place our faith in God and knew that was the best we could do.

After landing in Seattle, I went to nearby McChord Air Force Base where I was to leave on a plane going to Vietnam. I spent eight tiresome hours at McChord, waiting for an early Sunday morning departure for Vietnam. There were no rooms available in the BOQ, and there was no place to bathe, relax, or get some sleep. I sat in an uncomfortable chair in the noisy lobby of the terminal which was overcrowded with young soldiers who were also going to Vietnam. They were tired, scared and confused. The Army's system for processing Vietnam replacements was overloaded and insensitive. It was a terrible way to send American soldiers to war.

The first leg of the flight to Japan on a Boeing 707 took nine hours with a refueling stop in Anchorage Alaska. Our ground time in Japan was about one hour. The flight from Japan to Vietnam took another six hours. When the plane finally landed at Cam Ranh Bay late in the evening, I was exhausted, and checked in at the field grade transient officers' quarters. I wrote a short letter to my family and collapsed for a few hours' sleep. At midnight, someone woke me up to tell me that I could catch a ride to the Bien Hoa Air Base. I boarded a C-130 cargo aircraft and it took off just before dawn for a one-hour flight. There were no seats in the plane, so I sat on the floor along with thirty exhausted soldiers who had also just arrived in Vietnam. When we landed at Bien Hoa, the heat and humidity seemed overwhelming. I have vivid memories of the heat inside that plane as it taxied. It was not long before I became accustomed to that heat and humidity.

With my duffle bag in tow, I asked a nearby non-commissioned officer how I could get to the 20th Engineer Brigade Headquarters, but there was no routine transportation available. I hailed one of the many

Army jeeps that were dashing about the area and the driver was glad to take a Lieutenant Colonel for a ride.

It was 06:00 hours when I arrived at the 20th Brigade headquarters. The men were beginning to stir. I was tired, hungry, and irritated about the poor treatment of incoming soldiers. My morale was very low, and I was anxious about what lay ahead for me. However, a cheerful sergeant in the Personnel Office gave me a warm greeting and quickly completed my paper work, so I could get on with my business. The sergeant escorted me to the office of Brigadier General Curtis W. Chapman, the Commanding General of the 20th Engineer Brigade. The Brigade he commanded was as large as an Infantry Division, with thirteen thousand men in three Groups and thirteen battalions.

General Chapman welcomed me and invited me to have breakfast with him in the mess. I had served with General Chapman during two earlier assignments. The first time we served in the Research and Development Directorate in the Office of the Chief of Engineers where Colonel Chapman was the Director of the Developments Division. Six years later, Colonel Chapman was my boss. He was the Executive Officer for the Chief of Engineers and I was the Special Assistant to the Chief of Engineers for Planning and Policy. General Chapman was an outstanding engineer officer and an excellent leader. He was a true professional with a sharp mind and he was very exacting.

After a quick breakfast, the first real meal that I had eaten in about forty-eight hours, we walked to his office. Chapman got right to the point and gave me clear guidance about how he wanted me to run the battalion. Then on a wall map he showed me the 20th Brigade's area of responsibility and pointed to Bear Cat where the 86th Engineer Battalion was stationed. Bear Cat was a large US base about twenty-five miles southeast of Saigon. Then General Chapman pointed to My Tho, the capital of Dinh Tuong province, in the Mekong Delta. He gave me a direct order to move the 86th Engineers from Bear Cat to a new base near My Tho by mid-August. That was less than fifteen days away. The battalion was moving to the Delta to support the US 9th Infantry Division which was moving into Dong Tam, about eight miles west of My Tho. The Division Commander was anxious to see the battalion move closer to his base.

Not only was I about to command a combat engineer battalion in the middle of a very hot war, but I was to make a major move that would require a road march of about seventy miles through areas that were quite unfriendly. I thought of many questions, but I knew that you do not ask those questions of a general. He was the man to tell you what to do. It was my job to get it done. I knew General Chapman well enough to understand that there was no slack in his order. I never did receive written orders for the move but, when you get it straight from the top brass, who needs it in writing?

I went with him to his war-room for a meeting with Major General David S. Parker, the USARV Engineer. He was General Chapman's boss. Chapman's staff described the activities of the 20th Brigade's three Groups and of their subordinate battalions. The briefing gave me a big picture of the engineers' activities. That was the last time that I was interested in the big picture. At my battalion, my interests became restricted to the operations that affected the lives of my men. It was the responsibility of the generals and their staffs to worry about the big picture.

After the briefing, General Parker welcomed me and wished me good luck in my new command. I couldn't help but wonder if both generals were thinking the same thought that was running through my mind: "This guy did a pretty good job as a staff officer in Washington, but has he got the experience and the leadership to handle a battalion in combat?"

After the meeting, General Chapman introduced me to the Commander of the 34th Engineer Group, Colonel William G. Stewart, my new commanding officer. Stewart told me to go with him, so I got my duffle bag and we were off in a Huey to inspect several job sites. Flying over the Mekong Delta for the first time was a new experience for me. Water glistened as far as I could see. It was the monsoon season. After a long day we finally landed at Vung Tau, the location of the 34th Group's headquarters. I met the members of the staff, had dinner in the officers' mess, and excused myself. I wrote a letter to my family and took my first bath in three days. I had a good night's sleep.

The next day I met with Colonel Stewart and the Group staff. Colonel Stewart talked about the condition and deployment of my battalion and some of the problems that I was about to assume. Stewart had been the 34th Group Commander for the better part of a year, so he had a lot of good guidance for his new battalion commander. He was a West Point graduate from the Class of 1945, a graduate of the Army War College, and he had earned a Master's Degree from Harvard. I met with each of the staff officers and they told me that my battalion had a lot of problems.

ASSUMPTION OF COMMAND

Late that day a Huey flew me to Bear Cat where Lieutenant Colonel Clyde A. (Pete) Selleck, Jr. welcomed me. Pete and I were friends from prior assignments. We walked to the CP and he introduced me to the staff. They were anxious about changing from a known commander to an unknown.

Figure 5 Passing the battalion colors, L to R LTC Peixotto, SGM Meeker, LTC Selleck

The Executive Officer was Major Paul Fleri. The Operations Officer, Major Bill Garcia, told me about the battalion's operations and how the four-line companies and their twelve platoons were committed to projects at several locations around the Delta. The Adjutant, First Lieutenant George A. Smigelski, described a litany of serious personnel problems. The Intelligence Officer, Lieutenant DiGiacomo, presented my first comprehensive look at the intensity of the enemy's activity in the battalion's area. The Supply Officer spoke of the shortage of many critical supplies and the shortage of repair parts to support our engineer equipment. I do not have the name of my first Supply Officer. The Maintenance Officer was 1st Lieutenant Frank J. Schiralde. The battalion Surgeon was Captain Vega. The Chaplain was Captain Mills. The Sergeant Major was John E. Meeker.

That evening, Pete Selleck talked to me about the condition of the battalion. He said the battalion was committed on too many missions and unable to meet project schedules. Engineer equipment and vehicles were in bad shape, and it was difficult for him to stay on top of every unit, although he said that the company commanders were very good.

Artillery fire interrupted my sleep that second night in Vietnam. I could tell the difference between outgoing artillery and the incoming rockets and mortars. Welcome to the war!

The next day, 1 August 1968, Pete and I flew to meet the company commanders and look over a few of their construction projects. The situation looked grim. The engineers were working on construction projects that would be difficult to complete in peacetime under dry conditions. They were fighting the monsoon rains, mud, and the Viet Cong. The young officers were doing their best to get their jobs done. Morale was good.

*****

I assumed command the next morning Friday, 2 August during a simple ceremony in the battalion's compound in Bear Cat. The battalion's six company commanders, their first sergeants, and their company guidons were present. Also present were four general officers: Major General Parker, Brigadier General Chapman, and two generals from the 9th Division.

Figure 6 LTC Ernest D. Peixotto

Lieutenant Colonel Selleck passed the battalion's colors to Sergeant Major Meeker who passed the colors to me. The passing of the colors symbolized the relief from command by the departing officer and the assumption of command by the incoming officer. The Adjutant read orders announcing that Lieutenant Colonel Ernest D. Peixotto had assumed command.

Following that, Colonel Selleck received the Legion of Merit, the Bronze Star Medal, and several Vietnamese Army medals. General Chapman told the men that they had done a heroic job during the past months and that there was much to do under the new commander. Pete made a brief farewell address, then I spoke briefly.

After the ceremony, the generals and Colonel Selleck left in waiting helicopters. It was all over. I was in command of a battalion engaged in a hot war.

There is an old Army story about a change-of-command. Before the ceremony, the outgoing commander thinks that the new commander will ruin the organization that he has worked so hard to build. The incoming commander thinks that the unit does not really look all that good and he will have his hands full to make it a good unit. On 2 August 1968, I suspect that Pete Selleck and I fit those roles. Pete had done a superior job with the battalion. The men held him in high regard, a very important clue. On the other hand, I did not like what I had seen during my brief look at the condition of the companies. Later I was to learn that things were worse than I had thought. My comments are in no way intended to reflect on the job that Colonel Selleck did while commanding the 86th. He did the very best under the circumstances. Lesser men would have failed. The battalion received the Meritorious Unit Citation for its achievements during his command tour. If there was blame it was the commanders and staffs of the higher headquarters who had over-committed the battalion. Even as I say that, it is difficult to blame anyone when the demands of that war exceeded the resources of the engineers assigned to support the war.

After the change of command ceremony, I gathered my six company commanders and the staff in the CP and encouraged them to tell me about the problems that challenged them as they performed their missions. I wanted to know about our major problems as seen by the men who ran the operations. I encouraged them to "tell it like it is" and to not hold back. It was important for them to know that they could be honest with me. They gave me an excellent picture of the challenge that lay ahead for all of us.

It was obvious that the men of the battalion were working under challenging circumstances: poor construction material, equipment shortages, miserable weather, and enemy action. The battalion's extensive and heavy operational commitment at many locations was, without question, one cause of the problems. That situation would get worse as the 34th Group assigned new missions to the battalion.

The battalion CP, the Headquarters Company, and the 595 Light Equipment Company were based in Bear Cat. Two companies, Bravo and Delta, had already moved to Dong Tam to construct facilities needed for 9ᵗʰ Division as it moved into Dong Tam from Bear Cat. Charlie Company's CP was located near the village of Ben Luc and its three platoons were working at separate locations in Long An Province. Alpha Company had already moved to Camp Viking to prepare the new base for the battalion's move from Bear Cat. The Land Clearing Detachment was clearing jungles near Bear Cat. Some of the men and equipment from the 595 Light Equipment Company were attached to line companies.

My challenge was to provide strong leadership to accomplish the battalion's multiple missions and to move to Camp Viking in just a few days. Was I ready to do what I had been training for ever since I entered the gates of West Point, to lead engineer soldiers in combat?

ORGANIZATION

The 86ᵗʰ Engineer Battalion (Combat) (Army) consisted of four Combat Engineer Companies, a Headquarters Company, the 595 Engineer Light Equipment Company, a platoon from the 67ᵗʰ Engineer Dump Truck Company, and a Land Clearing Team. There were more than one-thousand men assigned to the battalion. The battalion had a vast number of heavy construction equipment: bulldozes, 5-ton dump trucks, cranes, front loaders, and much more engineer equipment. There were three platoons and company headquarters section in each of the four Combat Engineer Companies. Headquarters Company's organization included a heavy equipment section and a battalion maintenance section. The 595 Engineer Light Equipment Company provided the battalion with more bulldozers, POL trucks, maintenance trucks, graders, large scrapers for major earth moving jobs, heavy equipment transporters, rough-terrain and tracked cranes, and a lot of 5-ton dump trucks.

VIET CONG IN THE MEKONG DELTA

The Mekong Delta is Vietnam's primary farming area. Rice is the country's key economic commodity. The Viet Cong and North Vietnam Army units controlled vast sections of the Mekong Delta and occupied many villages and hidden bases. They were supplied from North Vietnam down the Ho Chi Minh Trail. Thousands of South Vietnamese civilians had fled from the Viet Cong to the cities, abandoning their farms. Those who stayed had difficulty growing rice and then getting it to market. Many cooperated with the Viet Cong either voluntarily or by coercion.

South Vietnamese Army (ARVN) units in the Delta were inadequate to defeat the enemy. During the TET offensive, the Viet Cong attacked Saigon from their sanctuaries in the Delta. Therefore, a very high-level decision had been made to move the US 9th Infantry Division into the Delta where it could carry the fight to the Viet Cong from a newly created base called Dong Tam.

Before the division could move into the Delta, Army Engineers had dredged millions of cubic yards of muck from the bottom of the Mekong River to create an area large enough for a division-sized base, Dong Tam. Then it took time for the silt-clay material to drain and dry before construction could begin.

It took an extraordinary expenditure of engineer resources to construct facilities in Dong Tam to house and support the division. Elements from three engineer battalions were committed to construct the cantonment barracks, roads, equipment maintenance facilities, helicopter landing pads, an airfield, refueling and rearming facilities, headquarters, laundries, a hospital, artillery firing positions, ammunition bunkers and storage areas, fuel storage, and so on.

FIRST ASSESSMENT OF THE BATTALION

My first full day with the battalion, Saturday 3 August, was a day I shall never forget. After a quick breakfast, I met with the staff. Major Paul Fleri and I studied the plans for moving to Camp Viking. The Operations Officer, Major Bill Garcia, told me about progress on current missions and the plans that were underway for new missions. The Intelligence Officer, Lieutenant DiGiacomo, presented intelligence reports about Viet Cong operations and the influx of North Vietnamese Army units. The Supply Officer brought me up to date about shortages. The other staff members discussed the maintenance situation, lists of personnel leaving and of those about to arrive. Those daily reviews with the staff were essential for me to be aware of battalion's situation, because it changed daily.

After a quick cup of coffee and time to digest the information from the staff, it was time for me to meet the men who did the battalion's work. To make wise decisions I believe that an effective commander must have firsthand knowledge about the conditions facing his men. Also, it is important for soldiers to see their commander and know he shares some of the hardships and danger with them. I believe that a commander who leads from his command post is an ineffective commander.

As my Huey lifted off the helicopter pad at Bear Cat, I saw a vast expanse of buildings, equipment, roads, barbed wire, fuel tanks, ammunition stocks, and the surrounding jungle. Bear Cat was a division base, an awesome sight, carved out of the jungle and rubber plantations. A reddish-brown coating of laterite dust covered everything within sight. Many of the Division's troops were still at Bear Cat, but they were due to move to Dong Tam soon.

Figure 7 Bear Cat

LAND CLEARING OPERATIONS

My first visit that day was with the Land Clearing Team which was working several miles south of Bear Cat, near the Binh Sanh rubber plantation. As my chopper circled the area I studied the large section of the jungle that the men had already cleared. A smoke grenade marked our landing site and showed the wind direction. It was SOP to land at an operational site only if a smoke grenade showed that the area was secure.

The Detachment Commander, First Lieutenant Charles W. Brisson and his senior non-commissioned

Figure 8 Land clearing Binh San Plantation

officer, Staff Sergeant Paul Spitkowski, met me at the chopper. Next, I met the man responsible for maintenance, Warrant Officer John McCafferty.

The Team's mission was to clear the jungle that a large Viet Cong unit had used as a base of operations to attack Saigon during the TET offensive. Lieutenant Brisson described how his men performed the clearing operation and explained why he was behind schedule. He described the security provisions that protected the men and the Rome Plows. The Viet Cong did not like the land clearing operation because it denied their cover and concealment.

I met the young infantry lieutenant who commanded the mechanized infantry company assigned for tactical security. His company was equipped with M-113 armored personnel carriers, .50 caliber machine guns, mortars, and other light infantry weapons. On call artillery units at Bear Cat were always available for fire support.

An M-113 took me a half mile to the clearing site where clouds of black diesel from the Rome Plows covered the area. First Lieutenant Ken Steen and First Lieutenant Barry Falkner met me as I climbed off the M-113.

The two lieutenants commanded the sixty men who ran thirty-five Rome Plows. A Rome Plow was a D-7 crawler tractor outfitted with a special dozer blade. The dozer blade's horizontal edge was sharp and there was a sharp vertical blade at the edge of the dozer blade. The operators used the vertical blade to split the trunks of large trees. After they splintered the trunks, it was easier to topple the tree with the sharp horizontal blade of the dozer. The Rome Plows worked together in an echelon formation as they moved around clearing the trees in the jungle. It was hard and dangerous work for the men.

A Rome Plows stopped long enough for me to climb aboard. I sat in the cab with the operator and watched

Figure 9 Rome Plow

20

how he controlled his giant machine as he attacked one large tree after another. That experience gave me an appreciation of the job from the point of view of the men who did the work. A heavy steel cage had been welded to the tractor cab to protect the operator from huge limbs and large trees that fell across the tractor. That work was much harder than running a normal bull dozer, because the operator had to keep up with the Rome Plows on his left and his right while he attacked one tree after another. The Rome Plows detonated many hidden mines and booby traps, and casualties were not unusual. It was dangerous work. The heat from the diesel engine combined with the jungle heat and humidity caused the working conditions in the cab to be almost unbearable. The temperature in the cab of the tractor must have been over one-hundred degrees. The operators drank a lot of water.

After an hour I commended the young soldier, dismounted, and talked with other Rome Plow operators. I admired them for what they were doing. They were a very special breed of men. Beside the Viet Cong, they faced dangers from the jungle: snakes, scorpions, bees, and red ants. Large ant nests fell into the cabs as their plow shook the trees. The men used smoke grenades to help disperse the bees.

The infantrymen and their M-113 armored personnel carriers protected the engineers as the Rome Plows cleared the jungle. The M-113s

Figure 10 M-113 Armored Personnel Carrier

formed a mobile defense around the perimeter of the work area and maneuvered along with the Rome Plows as the clearing operation progressed.

At the end of a long day the operators drove their Rome Plows back to the base camp, had a quick supper, and worked well into the night to take care of their equipment before they got some sleep. The detachment's maintenance team worked all night on some Rome Plows to prepare them for operation in the morning. While the engineers took care of their Rome Plows, the M-113s formed a defensive circle around the base. The engineers and infantrymen worked well together and had a mutual respect for one another. They both had tough jobs.

Colonel Stewart had warned me that the maintenance of the Rome Plows would be one of my biggest challenges; however, I was shocked to learn that sixteen of the thirty-five Rome Plows were out of action. A fifty-five percent deadline rate for a unit committed to an important mission was terrible.

When I discussed the problem with Lieutenant Brisson and Warrant Officer McCafferty, they explained that the basic problem was the D-7 dozers were not intended to work under the severe conditions encountered in clearing Vietnam's jungles. They could not get enough repair parts to keep up with the rate of failures. Jungle clearing was a high priority for USARV, but the supply system did not supply the necessary parts they needed.

As I was leaving, I told Lieutenant Brisson his detachment was doing an excellent job under tough circumstances and deserved my praise. I told him that I expected him to redouble his efforts to keep the equipment running and finish on schedule. There was no lack of leadership, skill, or desire with the men of the detachment. It was my responsibility to improve the support they received from the battalion and the supply system.

Figure 12 Ben Luc Bridge

As I flew on to meet with Captain Cidras at Ben Luc, my thoughts went back to my last duty assignment with the Chief of Engineers when General Westmoreland had asked the Corps of Engineers to help clear the jungles because the use of Agent Orange and napalm were unsatisfactory. Agent Orange was causing severe health problems for both US and South Vietnamese personnel. Civilian contractors with experience clearing jungles in South America had recommended that the Army adopt the use of Rome Plows. Lieutenant General Cassidy decided to use the Rome Plows, but, at the operating end of that decision, it was obvious to me that whoever decided that the undersized D-7 dozers could do the job had grossly underestimated the requirements for logistic support for the D-7 Rome Plows.

HIGHWAY QL-4

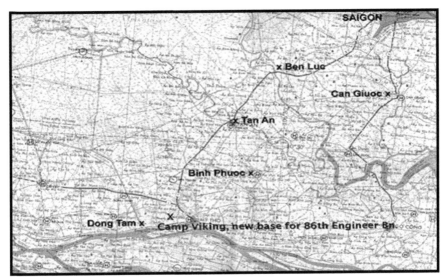

Figure 11 Area of operations

At my next stop, my Huey landed at Charlie Company's CP, just north of Ben Luc, which is about twenty-two miles southwest of Saigon on highway QL-4. Captain Joseph Cidras, the company commander, his company officers, and his key non-commissioned officers greeted me, and we walked to his small CP where Cidras described how his company was committed to projects at three locations. One platoon was at Tan An, another was at the Binh Duc airfield, and the third was clearing mines on highway QL-4.

*****

Highway QL-4 was the solitary highway that connected Saigon with the twelve provinces of the Mekong Delta and was of great strategic value because all the military and civilian traffic traveling from Saigon into the Mekong Delta had no other route than to use QL-4. However, the highway was vulnerable to Viet Cong attacks and interdictions that disrupted the flow of critical supplies. When the Viet Cong blew craters in the road and destroyed bridges, military and civilian vehicles backed up for miles until engineers repaired the damage. It took a lot of engineer resources to keep QL-4 open to traffic, and a lot of troops to help secure the route.

The paved two-lane road crossed over two large bridges and many smaller ones that were vulnerable to Viet Cong sabotage. One bridge crossed over the Song Vam Co Dong River at Ben Luc on a large multi-span through-truss steel bridge. The Viet Cong had destroyed that bridge during the TET debacle. Construction of a new bridge was underway by US civilian contractors working for the Army Engineers. Upstream from that bridge was an M4-T6 pontoon bridge, on which one-way traffic moved cautiously across the long floating bridge while long lines of vehicles on both sides of the river waited to cross. ARVN engineers had installed the pontoon bridge. I wondered why they had not installed two pontoon bridges for two lane traffic.

Eight kilometers south of Ben Luc, at Tan An, QL-4 passed over the Song Vam Co Tay River on another multi-span through-truss steel bridge.

QL-4 continued southwest from Tan An for 14 kilometers to an intersection where QL-4 turned west and the other branch went on to My Tho. The vital road continued west for about 35 miles to My Thuan where all traffic crossed the Mekong River on ferries.

Figure 13 Crossing on M4-t6 Pontoon Bridge

TAN AN WHARF

Cidras and I flew to Tan An to visit First Lieutenant Wayne France from Fairfax, Virginia and his 3rd Platoon. The hard-working engineers were

just completing the construction of a forty by sixty-foot wharf on the north bank of the river, about one-half mile downstream from the Tan An bridge. The purpose of the wharf was to unload barges that delivered crushed rock from rock quarries

Figure 14 Tan An Rock off-loading wharf

in the Vung Tau area. There was no rock available in the Delta and it is essential for road construction.

I was impressed to learn that the 3rd Platoon engineers had worked around the clock, 24 hours a day, to complete the project, which involved one-hundred and thirty-two eighty-foot long timber piles that were driven into the river bed with a pile-driving rig attached to a 20-ton rough terrain crane. The piles were necessary to support the thick timber deck of the wharf that was strong enough to support the crane that offloaded the crushed rock to waiting 5-ton trucks. After the platoon completed the wharf they unloaded the barges, another twenty-four hour a day job when barges were available. The men of the 3rd Platoon had also built a road to connect the wharf with QL-4.

TAN AN BRIDGE

From the wharf we drove back to examine the multi-span through truss bridge at Tan An. Two large concrete piers supported the main span, while seven structural steel piers supported the two-approach spans.

That vital bridge was a prime target for sabotage. After the Viet Cong destroyed the through-truss bridge at Ben Luc, the brass at the U.S. Army Vietnam headquarters was anxious about the security of the Tan An bridge. General Parker ordered the construction of devices to ensure that the bridge was not damaged. The 34th Group assigned the protection of that very high priority bridge to the 86th Combat Engineer Battalion. Protecting that bridge became a full-time mission for the battalion.

I talked with the commander of the ARVN infantry company responsible for the security of the bridge. His soldiers stood guard on the bridge day and night and watched the steady flow of buses, civilian trucks, US and ARVN military vehicles, motor

Figure 15 Tan An Bridge

scooters, and cars moving across the bridge 24 hours a day. A single barbed wire perimeter fence was the sole protection for the bridge on both shores.

CAMP VIKING

My next stop was the battalion's new base, Camp Viking. Captain Mouser, the Alpha Company commander, and his First Sergeant met me. We walked around the twenty-five-acre rectangular base, which Alpha Company had constructed. The long axis ran east-west. On the north side of the base I could see rice paddies, a small airstrip, more rice paddies, and some wooded areas. On the south side I saw a 40-meter-wide canal, which offered some security on our southern flank. Alpha Company was bivouacked in the eastern end of the base. To the west was an old base that an ARVN battalion once used.

Figure 16 Camp Viking

The entrance to the base was at the south-western corner where a one-hundred-foot triplesingle Bailey Bridge crossed the canal before the road connected to a narrow dirt road, TL-25. The 9th Division's Dong Tam base was eight miles to the west of Camp Viking, and the city of My Tho was a mile to the east. Just to the south of TL-25, was the mighty My Tho River, the name assigned to that large branch of the Mekong River.

Alpha Company, reinforced with heavy equipment from the 595 Light Equipment Company, began construction of Camp Viking back in June 1968. During the dry season they had excavated thousands of cubic yards of silt-clay soil from the rice paddies, spread the fine delta soil in six to nine-inch layers, and then mixed it with water to compact the soil. The final elevation of the base was a couple of feet above the predicted high-water level of the Mekong River that would occur during the monsoon season. Alpha Company engineers had installed a series of culverts and ditches to carry the rain water off to the canal and the rice paddies. Even so, the entire area was waterlogged from the heavy daily rains.

Alpha Company was bivouacked at the eastern end of the base. The men were busy constructing the essential facilities needed before the move: eight large personnel bunkers [twenty by forty feet], six guard

bunkers, five defensive fighting bunkers, thirty tents, four showers, five latrines, three water towers, and a 26,000-square foot sandcement stabilized hard-stand for battalion maintenance. They installed a 6,160-foot double apron and triple concertina along the northern perimeter.

I praised Captain Mouser and his engineers for constructing our new base and Mouser assured me that he would be ready when the battalion headquarters and Headquarters Company would arrive in two weeks.

Figure 17 Captain Mouser

QL-4 INTERDICTED

As noted earlier, highway QL-4 was vulnerable to Viet Cong actions to interdict traffic and disrupt the flow of critical supplies. Both military and civilian vehicles backed up for miles until engineers could repair the damaged area of the highway. The same night I spent with Alpha Company

Figure 18 Highway QL-4

the Viet Cong blew craters in the road and damaged the M4-T6 pontoon bridge at Ben Luc. It had been a big night for the enemy. As I was about to leave Alpha Company, I received orders to repair the damaged sections of the highway. I flew to examine two large craters at separate locations and directed Alpha Company to dispatch a platoon from Camp Viking to repair the damaged highway.

There was no doubt in my mind that the enemy was capable of a surprise attack at almost any place of their choosing. I stopped off at Ben Luc to see the damaged pontoon bridge and help, but the senior ARVN engineer reported that the situation was under control.

DONG TAM CONSTRUCTION

My next to last stop that day was Dong Tam. It was a short flight from Viking to the heliport in Dong Tam, where First Lieutenant Bernard W. Robinson, commander of Bravo Company and Captain Joseph G. Huber, Jr., commander of Delta Company met me.

The battalion's mission was to construct a 14,000 square-foot aviation operation building, four 12,000 square-foot vehicle maintenance buildings, the division's laundry, nine barracks buildings for the Reliable Non-Commissioned Officers School, several large hardstand areas, miles of roads, and many drainage culverts.

That type of construction work was a challenge for our combat engineers because their training did not include carpentry, plumbing, and electrical work; the project was more suited for a construction battalion. However, the men did their best and learned how to do the work from a few men who had some of the needed experience.

Figure 19 Dong Tam

Robinson and Huber drove me around Dong Tam to look at the work and learn how they managed the workload. During that inspection, I saw that their engineers were working on all projects at the same time. They spread their resources too thin to make satisfactory progress on any one project.

The mission was a top priority for Major General Julian Ewell, the Commanding General of the 9th Division. He wanted General Parker and General Chapman to complete the work quickly, so the division could move more units from Bear Cat.

It was getting late in the day, so I made it a quick visit with a promise that I would return soon. At the Dong Tam heliport, I exchanged greetings with Lieutenant Colonel William F. Lackman Jr., a West Point classmate. Bill commanded the 3/47 Infantry Battalion in the Riverine Brigade, which lived aboard several Navy vessels that served as bases for the infantry units to fight the Viet Cong along the length of the Mekong River. The brigade's mobility in the waterways was effective and gave the division access to an enemy they could not otherwise reach. Navy swift boats were also in the area. The 86th received several missions to support the Riverine Brigade.

34th GROUP COMMANDER'S CONFERENCE

My last stop that day was Vung Tau, because I was due to attend Colonel Stewart's conference. It was a command performance. I had no choice but to be absent from my battalion CP on my first full day in command.

The conference began Saturday evening with a brief social drink before dinner in the Group's mess. I talked with the other battalion commanders and members of the 34th Group staff. After dinner, I excused myself, wrote an event filled letter to Libby, and got some needed sleep. It had been a long day for me.

Figure 20 34th Group Commanders

There were four battalions in the 34th Group: three construction battalions and my combat engineer battalion. Lieutenant Colonel Ralph Sievers commanded the 93rd Construction Battalion in Dong Tam. Lieutenant Colonel Rich Leonard commanded the 35th Construction Battalion and Lieutenant Colonel Jerry Goetz commanded 69th Construction Battalion. I cannot recall where those last two battalions were deployed on construction missions.

The Sunday morning meeting with Colonel Stewart and his staff came at an inconvenient time for me, but it was helpful to me as a new commander. Bill Stewart was all business. Each construction battalion commander spoke about their progress, successes, and problems where they needed better support from the 34th Group staff.

When the conference ended, I attended a Sunday communion service conducted by the 34th Group Chaplain. I was thankful for a few moments to pray for God's guidance before flying back to my CP.

CASUALTIES AND SECURITY

When I arrived back at Bear Cat, Major Paul Fleri told me that the Viet Cong ambushed one of our squads as they supported a 9th Division infantry unit. Two engineers had been killed and another two were wounded. The news of that tragic loss hit me like a ton of bricks. Those four engineer soldiers were beloved by their families, and I was responsible for their safety and their wellbeing. Details about the ambush were limited because we had no direct radio contact with the infantry unit they were supporting.

On my third day in command I had the heartbreaking duty to conduct a memorial service for the two fallen engineers. I flew to Delta Company's CP in Dong Tam, accompanied by Chaplain Harrold Mills, and Sergeant Major Meeker. The service was brief but very emotional for his comrades and for me. The men of the platoon stood facing their fallen comrades' two rifles with their bayonets thrust in the ground with their helmets atop the rifles. Their boots were on the ground in front of the rifles. Chaplain Mills, Captain Huber, the company commander, and I faced the men as the Chaplain read several comforting lessons from the Bible and offered prayers for our fallen comrades. After my brief comments, a squad fired a rifle volley as a military salute. That was my first memorial service, but it was not to be the last.

After the service, I inspected the security of every one of the battalion's work-sites I could reach that day, to assess the battalion's security procedures for our platoon's work-sites and bivouacs. I had many questions. Was the security adequate? Did they have adequate training? Were their weapons close by and working? What were the standard operating procedures? Was medical attention available in time to help? Was discipline lax? Were the engineers in contact with the infantry? Did the engineers have local security?

Occasionally our engineers tended to become overconfident and believe they were in a safe area if there had been no recent Viet Cong activity; however, the Viet Cong were always present; no area in the Delta was safe. Viet Cong men and women watched our job sites, and if they detected a weakness in our defenses, they attacked. In addition to snipers, and ambushes, there were hidden mines, booby traps, and punji stakes, a sharpened bamboo stick coated with a poison or with human fecal material. The sharp stakes could penetrate the sole of a combat boot. The Viet Cong lived in nearby villages and gave us friendly greetings during the day, but it was impossible to know if an old man, a young boy, or a woman living nearby to one of our worksites was a friend or an enemy. Too many Vietnamese were not our friends. They acted friendly, but that was part of the deception. We could not exclude the Vietnamese from a construction site because we were working for their hearts and minds by opening the secondary roads needed by Vietnamese farmers to get their vegetables and rice to the market.

Our engineers were always responsible for their own security. Combat engineers are trained to fight as infantry. It is part of their creed and mission. At the construction sites our engineers kept their weapons nearby while they worked, ready to defend themselves if the Viet Cong attacked. There were many occasions when our men came under attack and fought the Viet Cong.

On a few missions, our engineers were able to coordinate security with a nearby 9th Division infantry unit. On a few other missions, they coordinated security with a nearby ARVN unit; however, Vietnamese security was never quite satisfactory. The language alone was a major problem. How do you coordinate security if you cannot communicate with the security force?

After their grueling day on the job, the men retired for the night in a base camp. I was pleased to see that most platoons constructed an earth berm around their base to protect the men from direct fire and observation. Beyond the berm, they placed a barbed wire and concertina fence. Inside the wire fence were claymore mines, trip flares, and other warning devices. Corrugated steel culvert-halves, covered with soil, protected the engineers during mortar and rocket attacks and a safe place to sleep. Engineers guarded the base twenty-four hours a day and used night-vision scopes to detect enemy activity during hours of darkness. I ordered all units to use that method.

I reminded all my officers and non-commissioned officers that they were responsible for the security of their men and their security was always their first priority over all operational matters.

*****

I spent that night with Alpha Company at Camp Viking to confirm that they had corrected the deficiencies that I saw during my first visit. That night gave me the chance to get to know Captain Mouser, his officers, and the non-commissioned officers. I believe that the better you know your people, the better your decisions will be in managing an organization. The most important decisions a leader makes are those that involve the assignment of individuals to the key jobs in an organization.

COLONEL STEWART INSPECTS

Figure 21 Colonel Stewart

On 7 August, Colonel Stewart and I inspected Alpha Company's work at Camp Viking, Lieutenant France's work at the Tan An wharf, Bravo and Delta companies' construction progress in Dong Tam, and the Land Clearing Team near the Long Binh Plantation. At each site, our young platoon leaders and their engineers were working hard to do their work as they overcame the daily rain and ever-present mud.

Colonel Stewart praised the progress but was very critical of the condition of our equipment, particularly at the Land Clearing Team's job site. It would have been easy for me to blame the problems on my predecessor, Pete Selleck, but that would have been unfair. I would not criticize the officer I replaced because I was not there to know about the challenges he had faced. These were my problems and it was up to me to correct them and improve the operation of the battalion. Our men deserved good leadership from me, and I needed to provide that leadership.

LAND CLEARING TEAM

Colonel Stewart and I returned to the Land Clearing Team on 13 August, because the clearing work was behind schedule and the "brass" at Headquarters USARV was unhappy with the battalion's performance. USARV wanted to start a new jungle clearing mission around Long Binh. The pressure to finish the work was intense. No one up the chain of command seemed to understand that a big part of my problem was a shortage of repair parts for the Rome Plows.

Lieutenant Brisson told us that they were slowly getting back on schedule for the number of acres cleared, although many of the Rome Plows were deadlined. Warrant Officer John McCafferty explained how he was able to place more Rome Plows in operation; however, the

Figure 22 Use of Hueys was essential to inspect operations

shortage of repair parts limited his ability to keep the equipment running.

I told Colonel Stewart that the buck stopped with me to fix the repair parts shortage. I was just twelve days on the job and needed a little time to correct a systemic supply problem that had existed for months. I knew that the problem began with the battalion's requisition system, which I had learned was full of errors. I accepted my share of the responsibility but asked for my commander's support. I needed less criticism from his staff and more support.

Colonel Stewart said that he agreed that Lieutenant Brisson and his men were doing the best they could under the circumstances, and that he would help with the supply situation. He understood the battalion's dilemma and agreed that I was on the right track and decided that he would have to trust me. Both of us were in serious trouble with the "brass." From that day on, Colonel Stewart was on my honor list of good leaders. I was not going to disappoint him. The pressure to meet the Land Clearing schedule was intense.

Next, we flew to the Long Binh area to reconnoiter the site of the next jungle clearing operation. That project would be difficult for my battalion to support once we moved to Camp Viking because of the increased distance from my CP.

A NIGHT WITH THE LAND CLEARING TEAM

My intuition told me that I should get back to the Land Clearing Team to study their operations and problems. Late that afternoon my jeep driver, Williams, Sergeant Major Meeker and I drove to the Land Clearing Team. Lieutenant Brisson was quite surprised to see me back so soon. I spent the night with the jungle eaters and sent Williams and Meeker back to Bear Cat.

The Rome Plows had already returned from the clearing site and were parked in a circle. It reminded me of the frontier days when the settlers parked their wagon trains in a circle for protection against the Indians. There were no Indians in the jungles but there were a lot of Viet Cong. The armored personnel carriers were mixed in with the Rome Plows to provide fire support in all directions. The perimeter was patrolled by infantrymen to spot approaching Viet Cong. Mortars were placed, ready to fire, in the middle of the camp and a few rounds of artillery were fired from Bear Cat to verify the accuracy of those rounds that landed near our perimeter.

It was a busy night. After midnight, the Viet Cong attacked, supported by their mortars. The infantrymen and the engineers engaged them in a fifteen-minute firefight. Finally, the Viet Cong withdrew and left behind five dead Viet Cong. There were no casualties to our men. Total Viet Cong casualties were usually unknown because they usually removed their dead from the area.

During the night, I had the opportunity to have some good man-to-man discussions with the three officers, the non-commissioned officers, some of the operators, and some mechanics. During each conversation, we talked about their maintenance difficulties. It was clear to me that the equipment operators were not abusing the equipment. The dozers took a terrible beating as they cleared the heavy trees. The maintenance team was doing their very best, working under the most difficult circumstances imaginable. Warrant Officer Spitkowski was doing an excellent job using every trick in the trade to keep the equipment working. Without his ability there would have been more deadlined Rome Plows.

I wanted to know if I was going to put my faith in the leaders or if I needed to relieve someone. I concluded that there was no reason to relieve anyone. They deserved praise and decorations for what they were doing in the jungle. They needed another heavy equipment mechanic and some very important tools. They had asked the battalion for help but there had been no response. My own staff had failed to support the mission.

The next morning, I rode in the cab of a Rome Plow with the operator as the powerful machine pushed its way through the jungle and swept the trees away in front of us. At times, falling trees and bamboo buried our tractor. The steel cage protected us from the large trees but not from the smaller debris and the bugs and snakes. The Rome Plow next to us hit a land mine. We stopped and checked for casualties; there were none except for our ears. My eardrums rang, and the blast reduced my ability to hear a conversation. The mine caused some damage to the Rome Plow, but a mechanic was able to get it back in action in a few minutes. I rode with other operators and learned how to control the tractor myself. I wanted to experience the operation of the machines and the men's stress. During a short break we ate a lunch of C rations and drank a lot of water. Later that afternoon after I had seen what I came for, I called in a chopper and flew back to Dong Tam.

*****

Two nights later, the Viet Cong attacked the operating base again with mortars, recoilless rifles, and rocket propelled grenades. During that attack, a mortar round hit the unit's ammunition bunker, and it burst into flames. One of our engineers, Specialist Five Robert L. Coon, ran from his protected position, through a hail of enemy shrapnel and small arms fire, to a nearby bulldozer. He drove the dozer to the bunker and covered the bunker with earth to smother the fire. Coon's personal bravery prevented many casualties among members of the Land Clearing

Team and the infantrymen. Later, we awarded Coons the Silver Star Medal for his heroic deed to save his engineer and infantry comrades.

MANAGING WORK IN DONG TAM

During another inspection of construction work in Dong Tam, Lieutenant Robinson and Captain Huber were still behind schedule while their engineers worked on every project at the same time. Their men were not at fault; they worked hard for long hours. It was up to me to make some management changes to complete the work on schedule.

I realized that Robinson and Huber had not applied the principles of construction management and needed help. I reviewed their plans and schedules with Bill Garcia and we developed a new work plan to concentrate the resources of the two companies on the highest priority projects to complete those projects first before moving on to the lower priority work. It was *Management 101*. That was exactly what we needed to do to successfully complete the mission on schedule.

The work at Dong Tam was so important that I decided that the two company commanders needed someone to direct the overall project. I told Bill Garcia to move to Dong Tam and take control of the operation of the two companies. With Bill in charge and directing the less experienced company commanders, Bravo and Delta companies were soon back on schedule, concentrating on the highest priority tasks.

MOVE TO CAMP VIKING

Planning for the move to Camp Viking had been under the careful supervision of Major Fleri. Once we completed the last-minute details for the move, I flew to Camp Viking and spent the night. On the way our chopper flew over a firefight between a unit from the 9th Division and the Viet Cong. I watched two Air Force jets attacking the enemy and I heard a few artillery rounds whistle by under our chopper. That would become a usual experience.

On Sunday, 11 August, the advance party from Headquarters Company moved to Camp Viking to prepare for the arrival of the battalion headquarters. I greeted them along with the men of Alpha

Company and more than four inches of rain. Camp Viking had become a sea of slippery mud. By the time the day ended, the mud-soaked clerks, cooks, and drivers of the advance party had set up their tents and established security. That evening the cooks served them a steak supper from a temporary kitchen in the back of a two-and-a-half-ton truck.

The Viet Cong attacked Camp Viking that night and engineers from Alpha Company and the advance party repulsed them during a vicious twenty-minute fire fight; however, the Viet Cong wounded two of our men. A Medevac chopper, from the 9th Division, took them to the MASH in Dong Tam.

*****

On the afternoon of 14 August, the men at Bear Cat loaded the last truck and prepared for an early morning departure. The move to Camp Viking used most of the battalion's 5-ton dump trucks and equipment transporters to move an enormous amount of construction supplies and equipment from Bear Cat to Camp Viking.

At 04:00 hours on 15 August, the long convoy of trucks and construction equipment left Bear Cat for a seventy-kilometer trip to Camp Viking. The convoy drove northwest from Bear Cat to Bien Hoa, through Saigon, and then turned south on highway QL-4 headed for My Tho. Convoy discipline was excellent, and the drivers avoided major accidents. I was concerned because accidents were common in Saigon and along QL-4. The convoy arrived safely at Camp Viking late in the afternoon. I welcomed the men to their wet home. The monsoon rains had lasted all day.

As the heavily loaded trucks drove onto the base, their wheels churned and spun in mud. In some cases, it was necessary for bulldozers to tow some of the trucks to their designated parking positions. I resolved that we must improve drainage and road surfaces to transform that muddy morass into an operational base. The men worked late that night and early the next morning preparing the battalion CP.

Headquarters Company moved into the western end of Camp Viking while Alpha Company continued to occupy the eastern end. That left an undeveloped area, about 500 meters, between the two companies, which we used for the storage of construction materials and for vehicle parking.

I received a message late that afternoon that both General Chapman and Colonel Stewart would arrive to inspect in the morning. I was not the least bit surprised by the news. The men worked late that night and early the next morning to prepare the battalion CP.

GENERAL CHAPMAN INSPECTS

General Chapman's chopper circled the camp before landing. I greeted them with my snappiest salute and walked them through the mud to inspect the base, such as it was. I described our plans for the development of the base and walked through more mud to inspect the defensive bunkers and other facilities. General Chapman talked to some of the officers and enlisted men as he toured the base. He was pleased with their accomplishments and said that he appreciated the dangers and the hardships caused by the move, but he added that there would be were many hardships ahead. The staff and the men had done a superb job. I was proud of them.

Figure 23 General Chapman

Major Garcia and I went with General Chapman to inspect construction projects in Dong Tam where the two companies were working to get back on schedule. We stopped at the Tan An wharf to watch the crushed rock unloading operation, and then went on to inspect the Tan An Bridge. Late that day we landed at the Land Clearing Team where Lieutenant Brisson met us and told General Chapman about their progress and the status of his Rome Plows. Seventeen Rome Plows were deadlined. Conditions had not changed much since Colonel Stewart's visit three days ago. Warrant Officer John McCafferty told General Chapman about his work to get more Rome Plows running and that the shortage of repair parts limited his ability to keep the equipment running.

Chapman said that he had serious doubts about our ability to complete the mission on schedule. I told him that it was the battalion's number one priority to complete the land clearing mission on time and said that my battalion had some serious repair parts supply problems that contributed to deadline rate. I assured him that we would fix that shortage as soon as possible. I told him that I needed some support from the maintenance and supply units in the 34th Group and 20th Brigade. I also said that the 20th Brigade had not authorized the battalion more mechanics, supply personnel, and maintenance equipment to support the Land Clearing Team when the 20th Brigade attached it to the battalion.

The general could have reprimanded me and relieved me from my command for speaking so openly. He did not. I had to assume that he put his faith in the battalion. That was a gamble for him because he was under pressure from General Parker and General Abrams to complete the operation and move on to a new project near Long Binh.

General Chapman dropped us off at Bear Cat where Bill and I managed to catch a flight on an Army Caribou cargo plane that was going to the Dong Tam airstrip. A jeep driver met me at Dong Tam and we headed for Camp Viking. However, the MPs stopped us; there were active Viet Cong snipers along the road to Camp Viking. Despite my desire to get back to my headquarters, we turned back and spent the night with Bill Garcia in Dong Tam. Routine travel along all roads was always hazardous to our health, but when the MPs gave strong warnings it was not worth the added risk. The next morning, we drove to Camp Viking after a patrol had cleared the road of the snipers and mines.

Back at Viking I learned that land line communications (telephone) with 9th Division had been set up. Before that, we were dependent on our radio. The staff sections were setting up their offices. The men were strengthening the defenses and adding some basic creature comforts. Mud was a big problem.

Soon after returning to Viking, I was off again for a day of flying to inspect all job sites and meet with my company commanders. That evening, I met with the staff for our usual briefings and then talked to Captain Ajer about his progress fixing our supply system. His report was encouraging, but I reminded him of how important that work was to improve the battalion's productivity.

CAMP VIKING

We had been directed to construct Camp Viking on the western approach to My Tho to strengthen the defense of the city. The Viet Cong had used that area to attack My Tho during the TET offensive. Our location made us a frequent target for the Viet Cong.

Figure 24 Road in Camp Viking

It took our engineers a month to complete the basic defensive system. Earth berms surrounded most fire support bases, but there was none for Camp Viking. Without a berm, we developed an integrated perimeter defensive system. Barbed wire and a concertina barrier surrounded the camp and was our first line of defense against a ground attack. A series of mines, flares, and other devices along that perimeter helped to impede a sneak attack and kill intruders. Automatic weapons mounted in the fighting bunkers along the perimeter covered the barrier.

The development of Camp Viking was an evolutionary process, because all the engineers at Camp Viking had full time duties and had little time to improve the basic facilities that Alpha Company had constructed.

In the beginning, it was essential to get the troops into tents and out of the rain. Tent canvas protected them from the rain but not from a direct hit. The tents clustered around personnel bunkers where the men could seek protection during mortar and rocket attacks. The men gradually converted the tents into better living quarters, called hooches, which were eight feet wide and sixteen feet long with wood floors and wood louvered walls four feet high. Two-by-fours framed an open screened area above the louvered wall, up to about seven feet, to help ventilate the tents which could become very hot. To protect the occupants from direct fire and from the fragmentation from near hits by mortars and rockets, they constructed a hollow wood wall about four feet high and filled it with dirt.

*****

We were not an island by ourselves. We were part of an integrated defense of the area with the 7th ARVN Division Headquarters in My Tho, and with the 9th Division. Most of our fire support came from the Dong Tam artillery, which enabled us to call for preplanned artillery fire at any one of the several pre-designated locations where the Viet Cong would most likely assemble and attack. Some of those preplanned target areas were set as close to our perimeter as prudent, very close. Harassment and interdiction fire helped to keep the Viet Cong at a distance. The artillery's 4.2-inch mortars at Dong Tam were the most accurate and reliable weapons. The artillery was on twenty-four-hour alert, so we could call on them to fire missions at any time of the day or night.

Figure 25 R to R Capt. Jones, Capt. Mouser, Maj. Garcia, Lt. McCloud, Capt. Dykes, LTC. Peixotto, Maj. Giambruno, Lt. Jones, Lt. Bourke

Occasionally it was necessary to call for support from helicopter gunships. They were on stand-by alert in Dong Tam and regularly helped defend Dong Tam and the division's remote fire bases. Occasionally we rated Air Force support. One weapon system that was very effective was Puff the Magic Dragon; a cargo plane equipped with mini guns that had a high rate of fire that could devastate a small target area with thousands of rounds.

I doubled the number of guards on the perimeter when intelligence reports warned of Viet Cong activity in our sector. I conducted practice alerts to train the men to move quickly to their assigned fighting positions. Every man had to know what to do and be confident that our defenses were impregnable. During those alerts, the officers and non-commissioned officers inspected every man to ensure that they were in the right place, on time, with the proper equipment, weapon, and ammunition, and that their radio or wire communications were working. After each alert, we evaluated our performance to detect deficiencies and correct them. The men did not complain about the drills because they understood that their necks were on the line. At Bear Cat, the men had lived within the security of a large base, and they were not directly involved in defending the perimeter. Now they were understandably jumpy. The practice alerts sharpened their skills and improved their confidence in their ability to defeat a Viet Cong attack. Failure would cost the lives of the soldiers.

Just before midnight, on 16 August, our guards spotted a large Viet Cong unit exiting the woods to our north and they were moving directly towards our base. They attacked with small arms, mortars, and rockets, and reached our perimeter, but our firepower and the well-planned artillery fire killed many of them and they finally retreated after a prolonged firefight.

Figure 26 M-42 Duster twin 40 mm guns

Two nights later, an intelligence report warned of another strong attack. The situation was serious. We could not be surprised, so everyone went to their pre-assigned defense positions. No one got much sleep that night and the Viet Cong kept us on edge. They hit us with several rockets, but they did not attack; no damage or casualties because the rockets were very inaccurate, thank God. I spent the next few nights sitting on or near my jeep because I needed to be outside where I could see what was happening. From my jeep, I could receive all messages and send commands as needed. The duty officer and the battalion communications section manned the command bunker 24-hours a day.

We needed more fire power to defend our base. I asked that the 9th Division Operations Officer for help. He approved my request and assigned two Dusters: twin 40-mm cannons mounted on a tank chassis. The next day the two Dusters moved into place along our northern perimeter where they had an excellent field of fire. Our engineers were glad to see the powerful weapons, and they welcomed the gun crews. Dusters are air defense weapon, but the Army used them as direct-fire weapons in Vietnam because there was no need for air defense in Vietnam. The Viet Cong had no planes and North Vietnam had no viable Air Force in our area of South Vietnam. The 9th Division also assigned an 81-mm mortar section to defend Camp Viking. A few .50 caliber machine guns appeared, the work of some midnight requisitioning. This was a common method of obtaining items that were essential, but not authorized.

During the early days at Camp Viking, there was an observation post on top of a large stockpile of laterite in the center of the base. From that vantage point the guards could see our northern and southern fronts. That observation post was a key element in our defense until we constructed two fifty-foot observation towers.

Guards, protected from sniper fire by sandbags, manned those two towers twenty-four hours a day and alerted the command center if they saw Viet Cong activity. A telephone in the tower connected the guards to the command center, which had direct connections to the Dusters, the mortar unit, the fighting bunkers, and to the 9th Division Tactical Operations Center. The connection to the 9th Division was our main link to call for artillery, air support, and to summon a Medevac chopper.

When the guards reported enemy activity, I climbed up the tower to take control the fight. Night vision equipment allowed me to see unsuspecting Viet Cong units at night and then direct the fire from the Dusters and the mortars.

Most attacking Viet Cong units followed a similar pattern. They assembled in the woods to our north and fired their mortars and rockets at our base. From the guard tower, I could see the flashes from their mortars and fired on them with the Dusters, our mortars, and some 4.2 mortars from Dong Tam. As they moved out of the woods moving toward Camp Viking, I could see them, using night vision equipment. They seemed to not realize that we could see them. As they approached our perimeter, our men in the fighting positions opened fire with the machine guns, M79 grenade launchers, and their rifles. Our coordinated intensive heavy firepower stopped all attacks and the Viet Cong withdrew taking their dead comrades with them. Too often, we suffered casualties and equipment damage from the mortar and rockets. Unlike the infantry, we did not bother to count the Viet Cong dead after an attack. We were not interested in the body count game.

A ONE-YEAR ROTATION

Figure 27 These guard towers were manned 24 hours a day

Officers and soldiers served twelve-months in Vietnam. That Army policy was very detrimental to the battalion's effectiveness and caused significant turbulence within the battalion.

The one-year policy caused me to lose close to one-twelfth of my experienced officers and enlisted men every month as they completed their one-year tour in Vietnam. Casualties caused added turbulence. Each departing man took with him a wealth of valuable combat engineering experience, and their replacements arrived with little experience.

Imagine running a successful business where all personnel changed once a year. What corporation could be successful if it fired or "let go" the men and women in the company once a year? The Vietnam war was unlike World War I and World War II, when George M. Cohan's song applied, "And we won't come back till it's over, over there."

Late in December our losses were especially large. That was a peak month and many men with January departure dates went home early for Christmas. Despite the efforts by higher headquarters to distribute the losses equally over twelve months, the personnel managers were unable to smooth out the peaks and valleys of the rotation program. We had several peak months when losses were extra heavy, and the company officers and non-commissioned officers had their hands full training and orienting new engineer soldiers.

During my year with the battalion, I lost one hundred and sixteen combat veteran officers as they left for the US and an equal number of officers arrived to replace those veteran officers. The continual departure of company commanders resulted in many changes of command ceremonies as untested officers assumed command of the companies. For example, both Charlie and Delta Companies had four company commanders during the year. I had to assign several experienced lieutenants to command companies because the personnel "pipeline" seemed to be shy of captains. On the staff, I had three Executive officers and four Intelligence Officers.

I found it necessary to talk with every officer and non-commissioned officer when they arrived to evaluate their potential to serve in various assignments. I also examined their files to help me decide where I should assign them. I weighed the needs of each company against each man's strengths and moved my best officers and non-commissioned officers from one unit to another to keep the most important leadership positions filled with the best talent available to me.

My basic policy was to assign newly arrived lieutenants as platoon leaders in a line company to lead combat engineers, learn the fundamentals of combat engineering, and adapt to the overall Vietnam experience. It took about six months for an officer to become an effective platoon leader. By the time they were good at their duties in a platoon, it was necessary to move some of them to command companies, and others to fill vacant duties on the battalion staff.

Most of my lieutenants were graduates of Officer Candidate Schools. I must insert here that my young Officer's Candidate School trained lieutenants were very good and that their instructors had done an excellent job preparing the young men to lead platoons in combat. Having been an Officer's Candidate School Tactical Officer myself during the Korean War, I knew how much and how little my officer candidates could learn within the ninety days available to train them. No Officer's Candidate School training can fully prepare a young officer to lead a platoon of men in combat, but they do the best they can within a limited time. Regardless of their training experience, most of my young lieutenants performed exceedingly well with the help of some very good veteran non-commissioned officers.

BATTALION STAFF

As the commander, I depended on my staff to manage the many details of a large battalion: personnel, intelligence, operations, plans, logistic support, communications, maintenance, and so on. The staff planned each operation to ensure full support for the executing unit. If a mission is not well planned and not properly supported, which is the job of the staff, it is difficult for the subordinate units executing the mission to succeed.

Figure 28 Command Post 86th Combat Engineers, Camp Viking

I could not have sustained effective command and control of the battalion without my Executive Officer, Major Paul Fleri, to manage the hour to hour operation of the staff, because I spent most of my time in the field where my engineers executed our missions. Every night, after I returned to my CP, I met with Paul and the staff to review their work, give guidance, and help him teach staff procedures. Paul, a West Point graduate commissioned in the Signal Corps, was a superb officer who served the battalion with distinction.

My Operations Officer, Bill Garcia, another West Point graduate, was as good as they come. He was an outstanding professional officer and he became my closest confidant, because we lived in the same hooch. I relied on him to prepare the plans for new projects that the 34th Group assigned to the battalion.

My other staff officers, products of the Officer Candidate Schools, had served as platoon leaders in the line companies before I assigned them to the staff. While they had valuable field experience, they had no training for staff work to be the Adjutant, the Intelligence Officer, the Supply Officer, the Signal Officer, and the Maintenance Officer. The young officers were bright and willing, but without the training, they were sorely handicapped. It took patience and time to develop each one; there were no alternatives. By the time they were proficient, their Vietnam tour ended, and they left for CONUS, causing the assignment of a platoon leader to the job. The 34th Group's Adjutant repeatedly told me that there were no qualified staff officers available in the personnel system, so we did the best we could.

The work of the Adjutant is vital because he managed the personnel and pay records of all the battalion's men as roughly 80 of them arrived each month and 80 of them left the battalion for CONUS. The personnel records are very important to each officer and soldier, even after the Army discharged them from the service. In addition, there was important paper work for casualties, decorations, emergency leave, promotions, and the daily Morning Report.

My first Adjutant, First Lieutenant George A. Smigelski, was an Officer's Candidate School trained officer; however, he had not been trained to manage the Army's complex administrative personnel policies and procedures. To his credit, he tried, but the complex paper work was difficult for someone not trained to handle it. Fortunately, the collective efforts of several non-commissioned officers and enlisted soldiers in the Adjutant's office helped him.

I badgered the 34th Group's Adjutant for several months to assign a qualified Adjutant to the battalion and, finally, the 34th Group assigned Captain Rodney C. Nutt, who was a trained Adjutant General Corps officer and was exceptionally well qualified for the job. Captain Nutt proved to be an outstanding officer and a strong member of the staff; he was an answer to my prayers.

The Intelligence Officer, Lieutenant DiGiacomo, and his experienced non-commissioned officers assembled intelligence reports from the 34th Group and from the 9th Division. Our best source of information about the enemy was the 9th Division, because its units conducted combat operations in most of the same areas where the 86th Battalion worked. We received a steady flow of intelligence about the Viet Cong and North

Vietnamese Army as they moved units, weapons, and supplies down the Ho Chi Minh Trail into the Plain of Reeds and then into our area.

The Intelligence Section's Reconnaissance Team reconnoitered areas where the battalion was to start a new project because the Operations Officer needed that information to plan the projects. The Reconnaissance Team collected information about the roads, the soil, construction materials, friendly and enemy activities, bridge sizes and their conditions, and a host of other details. The men in the Reconnaissance Team travelled in three-quarter ton trucks, armed with .50 caliber machineguns and any other weapons they could beg borrow or steal. That was dangerous work.

Lieutenant Di Giacomo was my first staff officer to leave for CONUS and civilian life. The night before his departure the officers gathered for a round of beers, and I removed (cut off) his name tag from his jungle fatigues. I attached his name tag to a four by eight-foot sheet of plywood that would serve as the battalion's honor role: those officers who had served the 86th Battalion, to include the officers who were killed in action. By the time I left the battalion there were one hundred and sixteen names on the honor role.

I chose First Lieutenant Nickerson as my new Intelligence Officer. He was one of the few college graduates among the Officer's Candidate School trained officers and had performed very well as a platoon leader. He was the best-qualified officer for the job, but like the other young Officer's Candidate School graduates, he had no training or experience with intelligence work. The experienced non-commissioned officers in his staff section helped him learn the job.

The Army did not train my officers to perform duties as adjutants, intelligence officers and supply officers. As a matter of fact, the Army did not train graduates from West Point and the Reserve Officers Training Corps to perform those staff duties. I first learned staff work as an Assistant Operations Officer working for a WWII veteran. My young officers did the very best they could, and I have no intent to demean their fine service.

Soon after taking command, it was necessary for me to select a new Supply Officer. While I had been working with the Land Clearing Team and the company commanders, I realized that the battalion's supply officer was not doing a decent job supporting the line companies and the Land Clearing Team. After examining the records of all the officers available to me in the battalion, I selected Captain Ed Ajer. He had been a company commander before my arrival and understood the basics of the requisition process. Ed Ajer had left his company due to a serious illness and was hospitalized, in-country. He returned to duty at a time when I needed his service as the Supply Officer. Ed Ajer was not enthusiastic when I told him that he would be the Supply Officer and I described the problems he would inherit. While Ajer had no training as a supply officer, he was very bright, and I believed that he could learn the work quickly. Fortunately, a new property book officer, Chief Warrant Officer Clyde Kennedy, arrived. He had an excellent record and was highly qualified. Ajer and his people vigorously attacked the supply problems and achieved positive results.

SERGEANT MAJOR MEEKER

Sergeant Major John E. Meeker was the finest non-commissioned officer I have ever known. He exemplified everything I could demand from a senior non-commissioned officer. His experience, training, temperament, and military ability were invaluable to me and to the battalion. I relied every day on John Meeker's competent advice and excellent judgment.

We worked as a team. He went with me wherever I flew or drove to see the work of our soldiers in the field. During my inspections of a company or a platoon, Meeker and I went our separate ways and checked several distinct aspects of the unit. I concentrated on operations, logistic support, equipment maintenance, security, construction progress and quality, and personnel issues. Meeker concentrated on the soldiers themselves by inspecting their living conditions, chow, mail delivery, leadership problems, and discipline. Meeker listened to feedback from our soldiers, the platoon sergeants, and the First Sergeants. He evaluated the non-commissioned officers' leadership while I did the same for the officers. After an inspection, we compared our findings and talked about the good and the bad officers and non-commissioned officers. On a few rare occasions, he discovered some performance problems by an officer. Meeker was not hesitant to make immediate on-the-spot corrections as needed. Working as a team, we did a thorough job.

Meeker and I honed our marksmanship skills occasionally by firing all the battalion's basic weapons: the .45-caliber pistol, the M-16 rifle, the M-14 rifle, and the M-79 40 mm grenade launcher. The men in our battalion carried M-14 rifles because the newer M-16 rifles were issued to the ARVN units. I liked the M-79 grenade launcher because it was a good weapon for engineers to defend construction sites against a hostile force. It discouraged many a Viet Cong caught sneaking up on our bases. The battalion was not authorized infantry weapons such as heavy .50 caliber machine guns and mortars.

MONSOON SEASON

Figure 29 SGM Meeker

One problem I could not fix was the monsoon season. It rained three to four inches every day for thirty to forty-five minutes. Occasionally, it rained all day long. The rains flooded the rice paddies, so, from the air, the only earth surfaces I could see above water level were the few roads, the villages, and the rice paddy dikes. My guess is that about ninety-five percent of the Mekong Delta countryside is under water during the monsoon season.

It was a challenge for our engineers to work under those difficult circumstances. The wet silty clay road surfaces were very slippery and dangerous. Earth moving projects with bull dozers and large scrapers was a challenge; however, priority projects had to continue even when there was so much water and mud. We were fighting the Viet Cong and a determined monsoon season.

The Mekong Delta is like the Mississippi River's delta in lower Louisiana and Mississippi. It was formed by the deposition of sediment as the 2,600-mile-long Mekong River flows across the Delta just before emptying into the South China Sea.

The many canals that connect with the river are water highways traveled by sampans transporting peaceful civilians and the Viet Cong. From the air it was impossible to tell the good natives from the bad ones unless they shot at us. The extensive web of canals was challenging to control.

BEN LUC FIREBASE

During the height of the monsoon season, I received an urgent mission from 34th Group to restore the Ben Luc firebase, which was one kilometer north of the village of Ben Luc and close to Charlie Company's CP. To the west was the Plain of Reeds, that vast expanse with miles of waist high reeds, which served as a sanctuary for Viet Cong and North Vietnamese Army units. It was their supply route into the Delta from Cambodia where the Ho Chi Minh Trail ended.

Ben Luc was an excellent location to protect Saigon and to fire missions deep into the Plain of Reeds with the long-range 155-mm self-propelled howitzers and 8-inch self-propelled howitzers of the 7th Battalion of the 8th Artillery Regiment. Those were the longest-range artillery guns in the 9th Division and they fired many missions supporting combat operations.

When I inspected the firebase with Captain Cidras, I was astonished to see how the monsoon rains had overwhelmed the inadequate drainage system and flooded the 1,700-foot network of roads and the gun positions. The movement of the tracked ammunition supply trucks and the tracked self-propelled artillery guns had ruined the saturated clay roads, degrading the unit's combat effectiveness. It was obvious that our job was to restore the road network and rebuild the drainage system at Ben Luc as rapidly as possible.

Captain Cidras agreed to assign that urgent mission to his 2nd Platoon. They worked on that project from mid-August to early November 1968. They installed more than 600 feet of steel culverts to drain water from the roads, following the first rule of a combat engineer, "get the water off the roads." Once they improved the drainage system, they re-built the interior road net, which needed the battalion's 5-ton truck drivers to transport thousands of cubic yards of laterite from Bear Cat, over fifty miles away, and many more truckloads of crushed rock from the Tan An wharf, about ten miles away.

They reconstructed the gun pads for the self-propelled artillery by first adding a thick layer of laterite, then 6 by 6-inch timbers to form the base for two layers of laminated 3 by 12-inch timbers on the top.

One night, the Viet Cong tried to destroy the base when they attacked with more than thirty-four mortar rounds, tragically killing one artillerymen and wounding six others. Miraculously, our engineers survived that attack unscathed.

While the 2nd Platoon continued their work, I assigned First Lieutenant Clay and his 3rd Platoon of Alpha Company to construct concrete

pads at the intersections of reconstructed road net, to protect the intersections from the turning action of the tracked artillery guns as the moved from one of the gun position to another, and as the tracked ammunition vehicle brought in ammunition to the gun sites.

Figure 30 155 mm self-propelled howitzer

Lieutenant Clay's engineers also constructed a concrete pad for the artillerymen's mess hall and built a bunker on the concrete to give them overhead protection enabling them to enjoy a meal without danger from incoming mortars and rockets.

*****

Very late one-night orders came from the 34th Group to assign one engineer squad to a 9th Division infantry battalion the next morning to provide combat engineer support. They were needed to detect and clear mines and booby traps and destroy the Viet Cong's underground bunkers. It was after midnight when I approved the tasking to one of the companies. That mission was like the one when we lost two men in an ambush, shortly after I had arrived.

COMMAND AND CONTROL

As I mentioned earlier, I believe that it is vital for a commander to spend as much time in the field with his men as time will allow. It was important that I be able to talk with my captains, lieutenants, and their non-commissioned officers and walk around the job sites with them to talk with their hard-working engineers. My job was to make my own assessment of their competence, job progress, security, morale, supplies, equipment maintenance, and more. That is why it was so important for my Sergeant Major to travel with me to check on those things that I could not cover while we were with a unit.

Command and control of my battalion was a challenge because our companies and platoons worked at many construction sites some distance from their company CP, and some units were 70 km from Camp Viking. Due to that dispersion, it was important that I have the use of a helicopter, a Huey or a Light Observation Helicopter, every day. However, the 20th Brigade had centralized control of all the Brigade's helicopters and I was dependent on staff officers in Long Binh to send a chopper every morning. Occasionally, the 9th Division helped me with their choppers when none were available from the 20th Brigade.

The brigade usually assigned a Huey, which was large enough to allow me to transport some of my key personnel, critical equipment, mail, hot meals, and supplies to the men working at distant work sites. When a line company's maintenance mechanics were unable to repair a deadlined dozer or other important items of equipment, one or two mechanics from the battalion's maintenance shops, equipped with the necessary tools and repair parts, went with me. Usually they were able to repair the equipment during my visit, but if they could not, I left them there and picked them up the next day. The mechanics did not relish an overnight stay at job sites.

Chaplain Mills was a frequent flyer because I wanted him to reach out to as many of our soldiers as possible; many soldiers joined with him in prayer, and to sing hymns.

Figure 31 Peixotto in flight in a Huey

Our chopper pilots and crews were some of the best in the Army, and I felt comfortable flying with them. Sometimes I needed to look at conditions on the ground in hostile areas and the pilots were willing to fly the chopper at low altitudes for me to see bridges, roads, etc. Occasionally the Viet Cong fired at our chopper and the two door gunners "smoked" them or drove them into tunnels. More than once, I looked down and saw the flash of an AK-47 aimed at our chopper. During a heavy storm, the pilots tried to fly over the storm, but the very turbulent weather caused us to turn back when it was obvious that the danger was too great to continue.

Whenever the 20th Brigade was unable to send a helicopter, my only options were to travel by jeep or stay in my CP. The latter choice was unacceptable, and I used my jeep, which limited the distance and number of jobsites I could inspect during a day. My jeep driver, Williams, my Sergeant Major, and I traveled many miles by the jeep.

Road travel was hazardous; there was a lot of hostile activity like snipers and mines along the roads. I carried an M-16 and rode in the front seat. The Sergeant Major sat in the back seat of the jeep with a sawed-off shotgun for short-range defense and an M-79 grenade launcher to reach out to a harder target. We both carried standard Army issue .45-caliber pistols. Williams had his M-14 rifle and drove fast through the more perilous sections of the roads. Only by the grace of God did we come through some situations unharmed. I still have one of the AK-47 rounds that lodged in the jeep. There was no protection from mines except for a few sandbags on the floor of the

Figure 32 Light Observation Helicopter (LOH)

jeep. When intelligence reported that Viet Cong and North Vietnamese Army units were active in an area I planned to pass through, a three-quarter ton truck with a .50 caliber machine gun from the Reconnaissance section travelled with us. That .50 caliber machine gun was intimidating and capable of reaching beyond the range of the Viet Cong's small arms.

LONG AN PROVINCE OPERATIONS

Prior to 1968, the Viet Cong had gradually gained control of large areas of Long An Province east of QL-4 and south of Saigon by systematically destroying the secondary roads and bridges to isolate their sanctuaries, which served as their bases for the attack

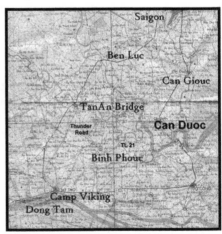

Figure 33 Long An Province operation sites

on Saigon during the 1968 TET offensive. The eastern sector of the province was not a very "friendly" area.

Many of the farmers that had lived in those areas deserted their farms and fled to Saigon for safety; however, many others stayed as virtual hostages of the Viet Cong, forced to provide them with food, shelter, intelligence, and transportation, or as willing members of the Viet Cong.

ARVN units had been unable to control the Viet Cong and few US combat units had been committed to Long An Province. The highway QL-4 corridor was

Figure 34 Planting rice

nominally under the control of the ARVN during the day, and the Viet Cong during the night.

In the fall of 1968, Colonel Hank Emerson, the commander of the 1st Brigade of the 9th Infantry Division, received orders to attack and defeat the Viet Cong in Long An Province. Emerson developed tactics to defeat Viet Cong units by detecting them from the air and quickly inserting his helicopter borne infantrymen into hot landing zones around the Viet Cong units.

Emerson's operations resulted in large Viet Cong body counts, which were significant because Secretary of Defense McNamara was measuring success of the war by the body count. However, the 9th Division suffered many casualties. After a battle, our troops returned to their fire base or to Dong Tam, leaving the area under the control of the Viet Cong even though they had lost the fight. There were not enough US, and South Vietnamese forces to occupy the entire province.

*****

While Dong Tam was the 9th Division's focal point to control the battle for the Delta, the division extended that control over greater regions by constructing small bases from which infantry and artillery units could conduct combat operations day and night, seven day a week. From those bases, artillery units could fire in support the infantry troops in contact with Viet Cong and North Vietnamese Army units.

The bases were as austere as any soldier has ever seen. In most cases, a protective earth berm surrounded the base, not unlike the stockades that protected Army forts during the Indian Wars. Encircling the base were barbed wire barricades laced with claymore mines, booby traps, and tin cans to alert the guards from a sneak attack. Inside the base, bunkers protected the infantrymen and artillerymen during mortar and rocket attacks. Also, inside the base were six or more artillery firing pads.

The construction and improvement of those fire bases was a high priority engineer mission. The 9th Division's 15th Combat Engineer Battalion constructed several bases, in great haste, during the earlier dry season. However, during the monsoon season, the rains inundated them, making it difficult for the artillerymen to move their howitzers, ammunition, and re-supply vehicles.

During the height of the monsoon season, the 9th Division called on the 34th Group to rebuild several fire bases. Of course, the 34th Group assigned the mission to the 86th Combat Engineer Battalion. Work at a typical base called for the assignment of one engineer platoon.

CAN GIUOC FIRE BASE

A good example of an artillery fire support base was Can Giuoc, which was twenty miles due south of Saigon on highway LTL 5. After the 15th Combat Engineer Battalion had roughed in the base during the previous dry season, a battery the 5th Battalion of the 42nd Artillery Regiment moved in with six M-102 105-mm howitzers to fire on Viet Cong targets on the southern approaches to Saigon and over a large area of Long An Province east of QL-4 where many of the division's contacts with the Viet Cong and North Vietnamese Army occurred.

During the monsoon season, Colonel Stewart ordered the 86th Engineer Battalion to rebuild the Can Giuoc firebase. I visited the base to see the conditions for myself. Thirty days of heavy rains had inundated the facilities. I talked with the battery commander, a young lieutenant, to learn what his priorities would be when we rebuilt his base. The living conditions were deplorable; they needed dry bunkers to live in and to protect them from surprise mortar attacks. The lack of a berm exposed his men to direct fire from the Viet Cong. Their situation was desperate.

The base was very muddy, and the entry road was almost impassable. The flooded rice paddies around the base made it very difficult to drain water from the base. Water surrounded the firing pads. Those conditions made it difficult for the artillerymen to perform their mission to support an infantry unit when it was fighting a Viet Cong unit.

I had no choice other than to order Lieutenant Robinson to withdraw a platoon from the high priority work in Dong Tam, realizing that I could be jeopardizing that priority construction schedule; however, the firebase mission carried a higher priority.

The 3rd Platoon from Bravo Company, under the command of First Lieutenant Dale D. Breed of Minneapolis, Minnesota, promptly moved to Can Giuoc and started work. The workload was too much for a single

Figure 35 Can Giuoc Fire Support Base during the monsoon season

platoon, so I reinforced it with more men and earth moving equipment from the 595 Light Equipment Company.

The engineers began by constructing personnel and command bunkers, reconstructing the access road from the nearby village, the interior road network, and they rebuilt six firing platforms for the M-102 105-mm towed howitzers. The gun pad design allowed the guns to turn and fire in any azimuth. That work called for enormous quantities of laterite and crushed rock to ensure that the base would be drier during the next monsoon season.

The delivery of crushed rock and laterite called for a coordinated battalion operation to transport those materials to Can Giuoc. We deployed more than thirty 5-ton dump trucks, borrowed from the line companies, to transport eighty truckloads of crushed rock from the Tan An wharf, a dangerous fifty-mile round trip for each truck driver. Also, those same truck drivers transported 450 truckloads of laterite from our borrow pit at Bear Cat, a one-hundred and twenty-mile round trip.

The trucks drove in convoys over the dangerous route through Saigon. Dump truck drivers rarely earn the title of heroes, but our drivers were heroes as they dutifully drove their trucks through areas where there was known Viet Cong activity. Tragically, several truck drivers died, and some were wounded when the Viet Cong used command-detonated mines to destroy or damage the trucks. Dump truck drivers of the 86th Engineers were fearless and courageous. The loss of a 5-ton truck to mines also diminished our capacity to haul vital material.

Using 595 Light Equipment Company's earthmoving equipment, they constructed a berm around the entire base by excavating silt-clay soil from nearby rice paddies. The engineers struggled under terrible conditions of mud and water. Under normal circumstances, an engineer would shut down the job, but I did not consider that alternative; the firebase was vital for the defense of Saigon.

Lieutenant Breed's engineers detected and cleared many mines and booby traps placed overnight by the Viet Cong along the supply road. The Viet Cong did not want the work completed because that firebase placed many of their sanctuaries within artillery range. One night, the Viet Cong destroyed a large bridge on the only road that connected the firebase with QL-4, thus halting the delivery of the crushed rock and laterite; however, even more important, it halted the delivery of ammunition and critical supplies to the base.

We needed to replace the bridge as quickly as possible. Major Garcia called the 20th Brigade to deliver a Bailey bridge. In the meantime, Lieutenant Breed and his engineers removed remnants of the old bridge and prepared new abutments for the Bailey bridge. Once the Bridge Company arrived, all the engineers worked for twenty-four hours to erect the bridge and launch it across the river. The rapid reaction to replace the bridge represented the collective efforts of the 20th Brigade as well as the challenging work by the combat engineers that erected the bridge.

Lieutenant Breed and his task force completed the first phase of the mission in sixty days under the worst conditions possible. While there were some doubts about the men's ability to overcome the poor soil and the persistent rains, the hard-working engineers completed their mission.

LAND CLEARING COMPLETED

By 30 August the Land Clearing Team had completed their mission, surprising my anxious chain of command, and vindicating the battalion. Action to beef up their maintenance and the determined effort of

Lieutenant Brisson and his men had paid off. The men needed rest from the arduous work and the danger before moving them to the next clearing mission around Long Binh. They were fatigued and had suffered many casualties. I decided to reassign Lieutenant Brisson, the commander, because he was showing signs of combat stress. It was time to get him out of there. His new job was Assistant to Bill Garcia in the Operations Section.

TRANSFER ROME PLOWS

Orders came from the 20th Brigade to transfer the Land Clearing Team to the 79th Engineer Group. The transfer made good sense, it was best for the 20th Brigade and for the 86th. There were no plans for land clearing operations in the Delta because the 20th Brigade staff believed that the Delta was too wet for land clearing operations.

The order required that I transfer thirty-two Rome Plows, in good operating condition, to the 79th Group. The orders prohibited the transfer of our deadlined Rome Plows, therefore I had no choice but to withdraw bulldozers from our line companies to send them north with the Land Clearing Team. I asked Colonel Stewart to intervene, but my protests fell on deaf ears.

The 79th Group was supposed to replace our dozers with good ones; however, that was a farce! It never happened. Many of the 79th Groups replacement dozers sent to us were inoperable. The transfer saddled the battalion with more deadlined dozers that added to our maintenance workload. Several of those dozers were in bad shape and the 9th Division Maintenance Battalion used them for repair parts. The essential point was that the battalion was short dozers when we needed them.

NON-COMMISSIONED OFFICERS

The Army's peacetime personnel system produced many excellent non-commissioned officers, and our battalion was fortunate to have many of them to lead our young soldiers. Their leadership was important since our young lieutenants had such limited experience when they arrived in Vietnam. Our veteran non-commissioned officers helped the new officers develop their leadership and engineer skills under combat conditions. As a 2nd Lieutenant, in Panama, I learned that non-commissioned officers were the solid rock foundation of leadership in a company. My Platoon Sergeant, Sergeant Packard, taught me a lot about leading soldiers. I believe that an officer must develop his leadership skills while serving at the platoon and company level.

Our non-commissioned officers led their soldiers and trained their officers under the most challenging combat conditions. Without their experienced, the 86th Engineer Battalion could not have carried out its missions.

It was my honor to reenlist several non-commissioned officers in the Regular Army. On Saturday, 5 October, I reenlisted the First Sergeant of Delta Company, E-7 Wright, by administering the oath of office. Wright was an outstanding African-American soldier like a large percent of non-commissioned officers that served their country and the Army with great distinction.

MAINTENANCE OF ENGINEER EQUIPMENT

The unsatisfactory maintenance situation was not limited to the Land Clearing Team. The battalion's deadline rate was deplorable; twenty-five percent of our equipment was inoperable. Too many trucks, dozers, cranes, etc. were deadlined. The lack of the availability of all our

Figure 36 LTC Peixotto re-enlisting First Sgt. Wright

equipment reduced the battalion's ability to carry out its missions. Using peacetime measures, the battalion was not combat ready.

Another "pain" was that the Army's table of organization and equipment for the battalion did not authorize enough mechanics for the maintenance sections of Headquarters Company and the 595 Light Equipment Company to keep up with the extensive use of our trucks and other engineer equipment. Also, the line company's mechanics were unable to keep up with the heavy use of the company's vehicles and engineer equipment. Their workload exceeded their capabilities.

The 5-ton dump truck, the workhorses of the battalion, took a terrible beating from constant use. Every day most of our truck drivers made a 120-mile round trip to Bear Cat to haul laterite, through Saigon, to the water-soaked job sites in the Delta. The battalion had more than sixty 5-ton dump trucks, but we did our work every day with about fifty percent of those trucks; too many of them were inoperable, deadlined, out of action, due to combat damage, accidents, and maintenance problems. Many deadlined 5-ton trucks awaited repair parts from the supply system. The same situation applied to our other equipment such as the D-7 bulldozers and the scoop loaders.

Figure 37 A 5-ton dump truck destroyed by a mine

Construction is a dangerous business, but more so in combat. Besides our combat casualties, several accidents killed or injured our soldiers as they worked on and around 5-ton trucks, bulldozers, large scoop loaders, rough terrain cranes, and large earth moving scrapers. One dreadful accident occurred when the driver of a 5-ton dump truck hit a hump in the road. The hump jarred the vehicle and threw the operator out of the cab onto the road. The medics evacuated the driver to the hospital in Long Binh for surgery. Later, after healing from the surgery, the medics evacuated him to a hospital in CONUS. Who says that driving a 5-ton dump truck in Vietnam was a piece of cake?

A 20th Brigade team consisting of several well-trained non-commissioned officers led by a Warrant Officer arrived late in August to help with our maintenance and supply operations. General Chapman had sent them, and they spent the day working with the staff. By the end of the day they gave me an objective assessment of the situation. They found many problems and recommended some solutions. They verified that some of our personnel did not have suitable training for their assigned work. The inspection was very helpful. I appreciated the help from higher headquarters.

Our mechanics worked hard to repair those 5-ton trucks and other essential engineer equipment to avoid sending them to the 9th Division's Maintenance Support Battalion, which was responsible to perform the more complex, higher echelon, maintenance for engineer equipment and vehicles. They had a staff of trained mechanics, proper tools, and equipment to perform the more complex repairs. Also, they worked in good maintenance facilities, which Bravo Company had constructed. Our mechanics worked in tents and the mud. The division's shops salvaged a lot of the battalion's equipment that we evacuated to their shops. They used the good parts to repair other vehicles. It was almost impossible to get replacement vehicles from the supply system.

I made a special trip to Dong Tam to meet with the Commanding Officer, a lieutenant colonel, of the 9th Division's Maintenance Support Battalion, to protest about his lack of service to my battalion. His excuse was that his mechanics and maintenance shops were overloaded with deadlined equipment from the division's units, and because the 86th Engineer Battalion was not part of the division, we were low on the priority list. I objected, and then demanded that he treat our equipment the same as the division's equipment, because we were supporting the division. He said that he could not change the priorities, leaving me with little hope for his support.

With little satisfaction, I met with the division's supply officer and the chief maintenance officer to demand that the 86th receive equal treatment. They said he would "do what they could do" to change the situation. It never happened, but I continued to complain.

Army regulations prohibited our battalion's mechanics to make the type of repairs performed by the division's maintenance personnel. When it was clear that the 9th Division would not support the battalion, I talked with my Maintenance Officer and with four of his best mechanics to ask if they could do most of the work done by the mechanics in 9th Division's Maintenance Battalion. They assured me that our mechanics were qualified to perform most all the higher echelon maintenance work, but they would be violating Army Regulations. Their only limitation was a lack of some specific tools available only to the Maintenance Battalion.

I decided that I must intentionally violate Army Regulations and authorize our Headquarters Company mechanics to do as much of the higher echelon maintenance that they could with the tools and experience that they had. I did not like violating Army regulations; however, they were written for peacetime conditions and I had an essential wartime mission to accomplish.

*****

During my inspections of the companies and their platoons, I realized that the chain of command had not paid adequate attention to the maintenance of their equipment. They had concentrated their attention on mission accomplishment, which was commendable and essential, but that was not enough. It was obvious to me that the officers and non-commissioned officers were not inspecting the condition of their equipment, and the operators were not performing daily maintenance, a sure menu for disaster.

The company commanders lacked the training and motivation to supervise maintenance. It was my job to motivate and train them. It took some drastic steps to get the chain-of-command seriously involved with the maintenance of every truck and piece of equipment.

I assembled a team of our best Headquarters Company mechanics and took them with me to Dong Tam to make an unannounced inspection of one company's equipment. At the end of the day, the mechanics had inspected all the vehicles and equipment and reported their findings to me. The results were worse than I had expected. The equipment was in deplorable condition. I presented the detailed list of deficiencies to Lieutenant Robinson, the company commander, and his officers, and delivered a very strong verbal reprimand, to use the words gently. I made it clear that I expected them to correct the deficiencies and start supervising the maintenance of their equipment. The company commander knew that he had little time to correct the problems or he would be relieved.

Later, I met with my other company commanders and gave them the same stern message. I ordered them to conduct daily maintenance and get their equipment back in shape or suffer the consequences. That day was a turning point for the battalion.

My next step was to teach our officers and non-commissioned officers how they should care for their equipment, because the Army had not taught that lesson to its officers and non-commissioned officers. Maintenance training at the Officer Candidate School and the Engineer

Basic Course was inadequate. I learned all about that subject when I was a second lieutenant in Panama, from the company's Motor Sergeant, a long-time veteran.

Shortly after the battalion's move to Camp Viking I met with the most competent maintenance non-commissioned officers in the battalion and told about my findings. I told them to develop a maintenance training course that they would use to teach the company commanders, First Sergeants, and the company Motor Sergeants how to conduct maintenance inspections and check on all types of vehicles in their respective unit for deficiencies and to conduct daily motor stables.

The expert non-commissioned officers conducted classes at Camp Viking for several weeks. The classes started with the fundamentals of how to conduct daily motor stables and how to inspect to ensure their operators were performing their maintenance. Finally, each student learned how to check all types of vehicles for deficiencies.

Soon after those classes finished, I began to see some positive results as I inspected the condition of our vehicles. Our equipment operators began to do a better job taking care of their equipment. I commended the company commanders.

I proved, once again, that the personal involvement of a commander is essential to the success of a unit. Early in my career, I heard General Bruce Clarke say that Asoldiers do well those things which the commander checks on.@ I know that is true.

*****

I received orders to attend an all-day conference at 20ᵗʰ Brigade Headquarters in Long Binh on 25 August for all battalion commanders. I cannot recall that my time spent at the conference was at all helpful to me.

SUPPLY OPERATIONS

The shortage of repair parts that had almost crippled our Land Clearing Team's work was not limited to the Land Clearing Team. It was the primary cause for delays in repairing most of our equipment and the cause for much of our deadlined equipment.

I had to fix our broken supply system because it was limiting the battalion's ability to perform its missions. First, as I mentioned previously, I replaced my Supply Officer, because, he was inexperienced and untrained for the job, although he was a very fine officer and a very capable platoon leader. I selected Captain Ed Ajer as the Supply Officer to use his leadership, management skills, and experience as a company commander to fix our supply operations. The non-commissioned officers in the Supply section knew their jobs, but they needed leadership and direction.

Captain Ajer and Chief Warrant Officer Kennedy went to work, and their first task was to audit our requisitions. What requisitions had been sent to higher headquarters? What repair parts were missing? They worked with their counterparts in the 34th Group and 20th Brigade staffs to reconcile old requisitions. They burned the midnight oil. They analyzed our procedures to detect where we were not following Army regulations.

His audit revealed that that there were many duplicate requisitions, too many incorrect requisitions, and many requisitions had never been prepared. The requisition process was broken. Our supply records were so inaccurate that the only thing to do was to cancel all old requisitions and submit hundreds of new requisitions.

The Army's supply system responded to the submission of requisitions prepared at the company level. A requisition trigged action to issue the needed part. It seems like a simple system; however, if a requisition was incorrect and did not order the right item, the supplies would not issue it. Likewise, if requisitions were not sent to the 34th Group S-4 supply officer, there would be no supplies issued.

The Motor Sergeants and the officers were not supervising their repair-parts clerks. Many of those clerks had not been trained to work with the Army's repair parts supply system. Consequently, they were unable to do their jobs properly. Sadly, many of the officers and non-commissioned officers did not know how the supply system worked.

Once again, I decided that it was necessary to teach our officers, non-commissioned officers, and company parts clerks about the requisition system. I told Captain Ajer to organize a course of supply operations at the company level and assign our best non-commissioned officers to conduct another series of classes at Camp Viking. Once they completed the training courses, I ordered all company commanders to prepare a new set of requisitions. For the first time, we knew what repair parts the battalion needed.

Once new requisitions had been submitted, we proved to the 34th Group that the supply system was not supporting the 86th Engineer Battalion. During our prior attempts to get help, the staff technicians showed that our paper work was faulty, and they did not take our requirements seriously. After doing our homework, the tables were turned. It had taken a lot of time and effort to train the officers, non-commissioned officer, and enlisted men to correctly document their repair parts requirements accurately, but finally the battalion had a solid basis to argue for help. Ajer and Chief Warrant Officer Clyde Kennedy slowly improved our supply operation.

*****

By a strange coincidence, Major General Andrew P. Rollins, Jr. visited the battalion in late September before leaving Vietnam to command the Engineer Training Center at Ft. Leonard Wood, Missouri where he would train engineer soldiers to fight in Vietnam. I used the opportunity to express my opinions about the quality of training for both the officers and the enlisted men.

*****

Another weak link in the supply chain was that too many repair parts were not available in the supply depots in Vietnam. I assume that the Army had failed to predict the quantity of critical repair parts needed to fight the war in Vietnam. That problem was exacerbated by the fact that the supply depots in Vietnam were unable to keep track of the repair parts that they had received. Many parts were in the depots, but those in authority did not seem to know where they were.

One of Ajer's non-commissioned officers had gone to the supply depot and found some critically needed parts, proving that some parts were available but not issued by the Depot. Ajer suggested that I authorize him to station one of his experienced supply non-commissioned officers at the Long Binh supply depot to find the parts we needed. I deplored circumventing the Army's system, but I approved his request because the supply system had failed to issue our needed parts, even for valid requisitions. I had to bypass the system to survive and carry out our mission. The non-commissioned officer had immediate success and sent the parts directly to the battalion. Our deadline rates began to decrease.

THE INSPECTOR GENERAL

One week after I assumed command, Paul Fleri told me that the battalion had failed to pass an inspection by the U.S. Army Vietnam's Inspector General a month before I took over command of the battalion. The inspection had resulted in a lengthy list of deficiencies that we had to correct before a re-inspection in October.

I was surprised to learn that HQ USARV conducted inspections of units engaged in combat, and that the Inspector General had applied peacetime standards to an over-committed battalion in combat. I do not recall reading about Inspector General inspections during WWII or during the Korean War. An inspection under peacetime conditions is a challenge for any Army unit.

There is an old Army saying, "There are two lies that are common in the Army. The first lie occurs when the Inspector General tells you; 'I am here to help you.' The second occurs when the commander of the unit being inspected says, 'We are happy to see you.'"

Failure to pass the inspection was unthinkable. I decided that we must not fail. I had to prepare the battalion for the re-inspection in a very short time, and that called for an enormous amount of time and effort by the staff and the companies to correct the deficiencies without degrading the operations of the battalion.

I realized that we had a lot of problems. When the Inspector General returned, the team would examine our supply operations to ensure that we were working in accordance with Army regulations. We were not. They would inspect to see that our equipment maintenance program was being performed in accordance with the book. It was not. They would inspect the Personnel Office to figure out if we operated in accordance with regulations. We were not.

Could any battalion in Vietnam staffed with short-term officers and enlisted men engaged in combat operations pass a "nit picking" inspection by the Inspector General? The deficiencies reported during the first inspection gave no consideration that the Army had failed to give us qualified officers, non-commissioned officers, and enlisted men to manage the battalion. The source of those problems went all the way back to the Army Staff, OSD, the President, and the Congress.

After challenging my officers, the chain-of-command developed an aggressive, command-centered, effort to correct the deficiencies. The officers and men did not panic.

Figure 38 Colonel
Graves Commander
34th Engineer Group

Many of the deficiencies had already corrected. As they worked on the list of deficiencies, they discovered more deficiencies that the Inspector General had not found.

The companies and the staff worked well together and there was a lot of cross talk between the companies. One company did not make satisfactory progress, so I ordered the battalion's maintenance and supply experts to work with the company and help them correct the deficiencies. Teamwork was essential.

Major Paul Fleri was the architect in transforming the performance of the staff to pass the inspection. Paul worked patiently with the young officers as they learned how to do their jobs. Late in September they paced themselves to be ready for the Inspector General inspection.

*****

As the staff and the company headquarters worked to prepare for the inspection, our platoons continued to execute their difficult jobs, and the Viet Cong continued to attack. A Platoon Sergeant was badly wounded by a booby trap. A Medevac took him to the Bien Hoa hospital. A lieutenant was wounded and treated by his medic. He was able to resume his duties. At Camp Viking mortar attacks wounded several engineers.

******

An intense engagement between elements of the 9th Division and the Viet Cong occurred on 1 September south of Viking, Kien Hoa Province. There were frequent artillery barrages and airstrikes. We were on the fringe of a major action, so we prepared for a direct attack. It would have been a major victory for the Viet Cong if they could overrun the base of a US engineer battalion.

The next night they attacked Camp Viking and our engineers fought off the Viet Cong. The men were itching for a fight and they were prepared. By midnight, the Viet Cong withdrew, and I sent most of the men back to their tents to get some rest because they had to be up early for a normal work day. I doubled the number of guards on the perimeter. Through a combination of training, planning and the proper weapons we were able to defend Camp Viking without any Viet Cong penetrations.

COLONEL GRAVES

Colonel Stewart made his farewell visit with the 86th on 4 September. We spent the day flying to most of our work sites. He talked with Lieutenant Breed and his engineers at Can Giuoc and they presented him with a VC flag that they had captured the day before. At the Ben Luc firebase, we talked with Charlie Company's 2nd Platoon leader and his platoon sergeant as their engineers labored to rebuild the interior roads capable of supporting the tracked artillery vehicles. It was during the previous night that thirty-four mortar rounds had hit the base, killing one and wounding six artillerymen.

Colonel Ernest Graves assumed command of the 34th Group on Sunday 8 September during a change of command ceremony in Vung Tau. Present were General Parker, General Chapman, and all four battalion commanders.

I first met Colonel Graves in 1956 when I was a student officer at MIT. At that time, he had the reputation as a brilliant officer with a great future in the Corps of Engineers. He lived up to his reputation and rose to the rank of Lieutenant General.

Three days after he assumed command, Colonel Graves came to Camp Viking to find out what the 86th Combat Engineer was doing. I had coached the staff the night before his arrival to ensure that their briefings addressed our most critical issues: operational missions, maintenance, supply, communications, intelligence, and personnel problems. Their briefings were hard hitting, factual, and quantitative wherever possible. The staff did an excellent job and I was proud of them.

After the briefings, I walked him around Camp Viking where he could see our living and working facilities and our defensive positions.

We talked about our maintenance and supply problems and the actions we were taking to correct them. I am a strong believer in General Abrams' guidance, "Do not hide bad news, it is like cheese, it smells worse as it ages." If you try to cover up problems, the commander will learn of them from other sources. Graves said very little as I talked, but he understood our situation and he improved support from his 34th Group headquarters.

Later that day, we visited the Can Giuoc firebase, the Ben Luc firebase, and the Dong Tam. Our engineers at those three locations continued to make progress despite the hardships and difficulties. The men's high spirits impressed Colonel Graves as he saw the difficulties they faced at each job site, and how the men worked to overcome them. Graves understood our situation, but he knew how to keep up the pressure, as he should. He was particularly interested in the maintenance problems with the 5-ton trucks and appreciated the importance of those trucks in hauling rock and laterite to the job sites.

CHAIN OF COMMAND VISITS

My entire chain-of-command descended on Camp Viking on Friday, the 13th of September, to inspect the battalion's operations: Major General David Parker, Brigadier General Curtis Chapman, and Colonel Ernest Graves. I joined them in General Parker's Huey as we flew to see the Tan An bridge, and the bases at Can Giuoc and Ben Luc. After returning to Camp Viking the staff presented our command briefing. The generals had lunch in the headquarters company mess, going through the chow line with the troops.

After lunch, we flew to Dong Tam to meet with Major General Julian Ewell. He told General Parker that he did not believe that my battalion could finish the construction work in Dong Tam on schedule. His units were waiting for the facilities the battalion was constructing. I was certain that the management changes we had made would enable us to complete the work on time, but I kept quiet because actions would speak louder than boasting. General Ewell wanted General Parker to commit more engineer troops to work at Dong Tam. The entire 93rd Construction Battalion, a large part of the 15th Engineer Battalion, and half of my battalion was committed to the project. Later, as we inspected our Dong Tam projects, I assured General Parker that the battalion would complete the work on time.

CRASH LANDING

That Friday the 13th was not without a serious incident. As we were flying back to Camp Viking from Can Giuoc a bullet hit the chopper. The pilot lost control of the rotor blades, but they continued to rotate and kept us aloft. Normally Hueys land vertically on the steel skids;

Figure 39 Tan An Bridge

there are no landing gears on a Huey. The pilot's only choice was to fly ahead and slowly lose altitude. By the grace of God and his great skill he was able to keep the chopper on a gradual descent heading for the only flat area in sight, an old dirt runway. As we approached the ground, we braced ourselves and I prayed for a safe landing, because it was highly probable that the chopper would skid along the ground, hit something, flip over, catch fire, and burn; we would not survive.

With God's help, our pilot skillfully set the skids on the ground and the Huey slid along for what seemed like a country mile before it finally came to a stop. God answered my prayers.

Once we were sure that everyone was all right, the pilot sent out a May Day for a rescue chopper. I regret that I cannot recall the name of the pilot. After so many years I have lost the names of too many officers and enlisted men who were associated with the battalion.

TAN AN BRIDGE PROTECTION

After the Viet Cong destruction of the bridge at Ben Luc, the brass at the U.S. Army Vietnam headquarters was anxious about the security of the other highway QL-4 bridge, the multi-span bridge at Tan An, which crossed over the Song Vam Co Tay River. That vital bridge was in danger of sabotage by the Viet Cong. Two large concrete piers supported the main span of the steel through-truss bridge, and seven structural steel piers supported the two approach sections to the bridge.

The 34th Group ordered the 86th Combat Engineer Battalion to protect those nine bridge piers from destruction. Captain Cidras and I assigned the mission to First Lieutenant France and his 3rd Platoon of Charlie Company. France and his men were already living just off the north approach span of the bridge next to the ARVN company that protected the bridge. Protecting that bridge became a full-time mission for France and his engineers.

The 20th Brigade's S-3 engineering staff designed the first of several projects to protect those nine bridge piers, a simple floating barrier to stop frogmen from floating explosives to the bridge piers. It consisted of 93 sections of hollow aluminum decking from

Figure 40 Main span of the Tan An Bridge

an M-4, Type 6 pontoon bridge, which Lieutenant France's engineers connected in series using two-inch steel cable. Once they finished that, they stretched the floating aluminum decking across the river from one bank to the other.

After Lieutenant France's engineers finished installing the floating barrier, General Parker and General Chapman planned for an early morning inspection. I left from Camp Viking, by jeep, before 07:00 hours to meet Generals Parker and Chapman. Early morning trips on QL-4 were a bit risky because engineers had not yet cleared the mines, and snipers were known to watch that road. A sniper shot one of my officers while traveling that way. Fortunately, we did not set off any mines, and there were no snipers.

After the generals landed and had the opportunity to examine the floating barriers, one upstream and one downstream, Captain Cidras explained how his engineers had connected the aluminum bridge parts together and anchored the booms on either bank of the river. Cidras pointed out the limited value of the barrier in preventing Viet Cong frogmen from going under the barrier with massive quantities of explosives. The two generals agreed that while it was of some help, it could not prevent the destruction of the bridge piers, so General Chapman put his staff to work designing better protective structures.

That floating barrier was just the first of many projects designed by the 20th Brigade's S-3 section. As soon as Lieutenant France's engineers completed one project, the 20th Brigade sent a design for another protective system. I reinforced Charlie Company with more men and equipment as the projects became more complicated.

*****

The Viet Cong tried several times to destroy the bridge. During one attempt, Viet Cong frogmen swam under the mine boom and struggled to place more than 2,000 pounds of explosives on the two concrete bridge piers. An alert Charlie Company guard saw the frogmen and warned everyone. He and others killed all the frogmen and captured the explosives without any damage to the bridge. To make it unhealthy for Viet Cong intruders, the ARVN guards occasionally dropped concussion grenades into the water around the bridge. They also fished that way.

*****

The bridge was of prime importance and a concern for many. One day the 34th Group notified me that a general officer had flown over the bridge and saw the mine booms were not in place. I called the acting company commander to close the booms and meet me at the bridge. With no chopper available, Meeker, my driver, and I drove as fast as possible to Tan An. When I arrived, the booms were back in place, so

I called Bill Garcia on my radio and told him to report that fact to the 34th Group. Captain Cidras was in Hawaii on a well-earned R&R, and he was due back from Hawaii the next morning. I reprimanded the acting company commander and the platoon leader, for their negligence.

Figure 41 Protective structure around one of the two concrete piers the hold the main span of the Tan An Bridge

That incident proved to me that even the simplest "screw ups" could result in disaster. I remembered the story of the German engineers who did not destroy the Ludendorff Bridge (often referred to as the Remagen Bridge) across the Rhine River during World War II. That one error gave the US Army 9ᵗʰ Armored Division of the First US Army a chance to cross the Rhine and establish a bridgehead on the east bank of the Rhine, and that changed General Eisenhower's plans to end the war. If the Tan An bridge had been destroyed, the 86ᵗʰ would become famous for the wrong reason.

*****

Shortly after returning to Camp Viking that evening, I received a report that Charlie Company's mechanics were unable to start the diesel generator that generated the electricity for the forty-one floodlights that illuminated the surface of the mine barriers and the bridge piers. The bridge was dark, and the bridge guards could see the mine booms.

I ordered the Headquarters Company commander to send his best diesel mechanics to repair the generator. It was a dark and a risky trip. I had to weigh the loss of the bridge versus the danger of ordering my men to embark on a very dangerous trip up QL-4. To ensure the mechanics safety, I dispatched one of the S-2 recon teams in their armed three-quarter ton truck to escort the mechanics. They arrived safely at Tan An and the mechanics succeeded in repairing the generator. The lights were back on. I breathed a sigh of relief and thanked God. I ordered the mechanics and the S-2 team to stay overnight with Lieutenant France's platoon at the bridge and return in the morning. That incident was just one of hundreds where men of the battalion risk their lives to carry out important missions.

*****

The 20ᵗʰ Brigade's final design to protect the bridge required that we construct a chain link fence, above and below the water level, around the nine piers. The complexity of that new project called for the commitment of more resources and the 34ᵗʰ Group provided five steel work barges along with welders and divers from the 523ʳᵈ Engineer Port Construction Company. The men from Charlie Company and the 523ʳᵈ went to work as a well-integrated team under the leadership of Lieutenant France.

During the first phase of the project, a pile driver mounted on a barge drove more than one-hundred steel I-beams piles around the bridge piers about three feet apart, and 30 meters from the bridge piers. During the next phase, men from the 3ʳᵈ Platoon and the 523ʳᵈ welded cross-bracing between every pile. Once the piles and cross bracing were in place, the men wrapped chain link fencing around the piles that surrounded each one of the piers. The top of the fence was about eight feet above the water line and the bottom was about ten feet underwater. Divers attached the chain link fence below the water level. The finished fence could prevent damage to the piers if the Viet Cong did succeed in detonating a large explosive device on the fence.

In anticipation of a worst-case scenario, if the bridge were damaged, Charlie Company constructed approach roads on both shores for an

Figure 42 "Brass" inspects Tan An Bridge L to R LTC. Peixotto, Col. Graves, Col. Parfitt, Capt. Cidras, General Parker

emergency pontoon bridge crossing site. The road on the north bank crossed a low marsh area, which called for a lot of fill material, which our 5-Ton truck drives hauled from the laterite pit at Bear Cat. The last step was to install bridle cables to hold a float bridge in case they emplaced a bridge.

I believe that we saved the bridge from destruction because we were always working on a new project. That kept the Viet Cong off guard. The battalion was always under the gun to ensure the security of that bridge. France spent most of his year in Vietnam working on that bridge project. That continuity and his outstanding leadership contributed to the success of his mission. More senior officers inspected his job site than visited any other job in the battalion.

LIEUTENANT COLONEL JESTER

Lieutenant Colonel Guy E. Jester commanded the 15th Combat Engineer Battalion of the 9th Infantry Division. Jester was responsible to General Ewell for coordinating engineer activities supporting the division, including my battalion. Although Colonel Graves was my commander, he recognized that

Figure 43 Examining Route 231 before work began

I should respond to top priority tasks directed by the 9th Division. Guy and I worked as a team. It helped that we were friends and West Point classmates. The two of us had one goal in mind and that was to execute the engineer missions of the 9th Division.

General Ewell delegated the supervision of the engineers to Brigadier General James S. Timothy, the Assistant Division Commander. Jester and I met with General Timothy from time to time to coordinate our operations with the division's overall battle plan. General Timothy helped clarify the responsibilities and missions of our respective battalions and the meetings helped ensure that the division's leadership understood my battalion's commitments.

ROUTE 231

The Long An Province road improvement program included a continuous series of projects to open one secondary road after the other. Restoring the use of those long unused roads was necessary to extend the 9th Division's control of the province and enable the local farmers to travel and transport their goods to the market.

The first of several such missions occurred when the 34th Group tasked the battalion to rebuild eight kilometers of Route 231, a nondescript road, which connected Binh Chan on highway QL-4 to a rural area that had become a Viet Cong sanctuary, much to close to Saigon. It was a priority mission to drive the Viet Cong out of that area because they were a continuing threat to the capital city.

Flying very low along Route 231 in a light observation helicopter, I saw the terrible condition of the road. It was impassable and flanked by unused inundated rice paddies and marshland. There was no way to bypass the road because of the surrounding rice paddies. Several segments of the road were nonexistent. Where there had been something like a road, there were deep trench-like holes about 250 feet long full of water. The Viet Cong had forced the local Vietnamese civilians to dig those holes and destroy the road. The monsoon rains had done the rest of the damage. In peacetime, given the weather conditions it would be asinine to tackle a project like that, but we had no choice but to go at it with gusto and figure out how to do the impossible.

I assigned that mission to First Lieutenant Brown and his 1st Platoon of Charlie Company. The platoon's base camp was three kilometers east of QL-4, and they received logistic support directly from Charlie Company's base at Ben Luc. The 2nd Battalion of the 47th Mechanized Infantry Regiment was fighting Viet Cong units in the area and offered some security for the engineers.

The 1st Platoon's engineers pumped as much water as possible from the huge holes in the roadbed with our limited pumping capability. Filling those deep long holes presented a major challenge because the remaining liquidized silty-clay material acted more like quick-sand. Lieutenant Brown's engineers used an unorthodox method to backfill the holes. First, they placed steel landing mat in the bottom of the holes and then they filled the holes with laterite transported from Bear Cat by our 5-ton truck drivers. Fortunately, the expedient unorthodox procedure worked; however, that solution does not appear in textbooks. The landing mat gave enough load bearing capability for the laterite. The platoon completed the road using their dozers and many more 5-ton truck loads of laterite hauled from Bear Cat.

The Viet Cong did their best to stop the work, but the infantrymen and the engineers repulsed them. During that operation, the platoon's men detected and removed seventy-six booby traps and many mines, which the Viet Cong planted every night.

ROUTE X

No sooner had Lieutenant Brown and his men completed work on Route 231, the 9th Division required the battalion to rebuild another rural road in Long An Province, Route X. The Viet Cong had all but ended traces of that road.

I tried to examine the condition of the road on the ground but that proved to be an impossible task. About fifty yards into the deep muddy road, it virtually disappeared, so I reconnoitered Route X from the air. It was very similar to the condition I saw on Route 231. I assigned the mission to Charlie Company because it was closest to their CP. First Lieutenant Brown and his 1st Platoon successfully completed work on Route X after two weeks on the job.

INSPECTOR GENERAL

I attended Chaplain Mills' chapel service every Sunday and always prayed for my men and my family; however, on that Sunday morning, 6 October, before the inspection I asked the Lord to help the battalion pass the inspection. I needed His help and I always turn to Him. One of my favorite Psalms goes like this, "In my distress I called upon the Lord, and he answered me." During the rest of that Sunday, everyone in the battalion checked many details as they made their final preparations. Tension was very high. Our officers, non-commissioned officers, and enlisted men had worked very hard.

On 7 October, two months after assuming command of the battalion, an inspection team of six Warrant Officers and several senior non-commissioned officers from the office of the U.S. Army Vietnam's Inspector General's office arrived at Camp Viking to re-inspect the 86th. They were experts in Army regulations and had a vast amount of experience in their technical fields. I met and welcomed them, and then released them to perform a very detailed inspection of all functional areas. There was no way to pull the wool over their eyes. They poked their noses into everything at Camp Viking and a few of them even braved visiting several job sites.

Late on the second day, the Team Chief came to me and said that the inspection had gone well. Captain Ajer's supply operations, which had been a disaster at the first inspection, were in proper shape. There were still a few deficiencies in the maintenance area, but the Team Chief acknowledged that the battalion knew about the problems and had taken proper action to correct the deficiencies. During an IG inspection, it is essential to prove that you know what is wrong, and that you have documentation to prove that you have action underway to correct the deficiencies. Captain Nutt's Adjutant's functions were in very good condition.

Once the team left Camp Viking, members of the battalion staff told me that their counterparts on the inspection team said that the inspection had gone well with a few minor deficiencies that were corrected within twenty-four hours. The departing comments encouraged us; however, I could not relax until I received the official report.

On Friday, 11 October, the inspection team returned to present a formal briefing on the results of the inspection; there were no major deficiencies in any functional area. They said that we passed! That was great news for the officers and men of the battalion; a great reason for them to celebrate. I was very pleased with them and told them so.

A month later, the official Inspector General's report, signed by an unknown general officer, confirmed that the battalion had no major deficiencies. However, the closing paragraph of the report alleged that that the battalion "lacked command concern." Those three words were an insult to me and my officers as well as to Colonel Graves and Colonel Parfitt! But most of all, it was a direct condemnation of my leadership. I was furious! I believe that the allegation was unwarranted and unjustified. It is not easy to raise my temper, but that report did. That allegation was false. It was a lie. Nothing could have been further from the truth, and I knew it and my officers knew it. The battalion's chain of command and the men had done an excellent job under adverse circumstances. The Team Chief complimented the officers and men of the battalion for a good showing. I was furious with the Inspector General in his comfortable U. S. Army Vietnam's headquarters living in air-conditioned quarters comfortably isolated from the realities of the war. I could not help but thinking "Was I fighting the enemy or the U.S. Army Vietnam's Inspector General?"

I talked to Colonel Graves about the Inspector General's report and he congratulated us on passing the tough inspection and assured me that he knew that the battalion did not lack for command interest and involvement and that the report was off base.

With the completion of that inspection, there was a temptation for the battalion's officers to relax. However, I believed that it was important that we continue to improve our many administrative functions. The inspection had been a good warning that conditions can go bad in a hurry if we let up on our efforts to improve the battalion's operations. To ensure that the men were doing their jobs I started a series of monthly inspections of each company by the technical experts on the battalion staff. The inspections proved to be very beneficial for the company commanders.

*****

There were more casualties as we took on more missions. A booby trap explosion badly wounded on engineer and a Medevac chopper took him to the hospital in Bien Hoa. The Viet Cong wounded a lieutenant and after the medic treated his wounds, he was able to resume his duties. At Camp Viking, mortar attacks wounded several engineers.

During the night of 8 October, units from the 7th ARVN Division were engaged in a major battle with a Viet Cong or a North Vietnamese Army unit about three miles north of Camp Viking. It was good to know that those enemy units were not able to reach our position. Also, there was a B-52 bomb strike on the enemy somewhere nearby and the bombs were so close that the earth trembled at Camp Viking. During that fight, the Viet Cong damaged the Ben Luc pontoon bridge again. I breathed a deep sigh of relief when I learned that the Tan An bridge was untouched.

VUNG TAU MEETING

Colonel Graves summoned his four battalion commanders to Vung Tau on the weekend of 12 and 13 October. The best part of the conference was a hot shower and a good night's sleep in an air-conditioned room.

Figure 44 Col. Graves and his battalion commanders and executive officer

Colonel Graves's style of leadership ensured strong management and control of his Group. He listened quietly, and when he did not like something he was quick to say so. He left no doubt about it. Graves discussed his priorities for the Group, many issues, and the other work that General Chapman was about to assign to the Group.

I listened to his staff officers talk about their activities, but I heard nothing new or facts that would have an important impact on my men. Due to distances and lack of choppers, both the Brigade's the Group's staffs were unable to visit the subordinate units to appreciate conditions in the field. That was also true for my own staff. That was the reason for the commander to spend his time with his subordinate units. Occasionally, it seemed to me that the staffs were deciding things in a vacuum. Commanders conferences helped to keep the staff informed about the real world at the battalion and company level.

COMMAND TOUR POLICY

One battalion commander was about to transfer to staff job at Long Binh after commanding his battalion for six months. I envied him because a staff job in Long Binh would be a relief from the stress of command; however, I did not want to leave my battalion after six months because I believed it would be detrimental to a battalion to change commanders every six months. The more experienced I gained, the more competent I believe I could lead and manage my more than one-thousand engineers.

During the Vietnam War, the Army's policy was to assign lieutenant colonels as battalion commanders for six months and then transfer them to a staff assignment to provide more officers with the opportunity to have combat command experience. I believe that was a bad policy because continuity is essential for commanders, particularly when one twelfth of the men left every month. Command in combat is far too important to use for career development. I believe that the six-month command policy resulted in a degradation of many units' performance.

I told Colonel Graves that I did not want to rotate after six months as a commander. He did not promise anything, but I did command the battalion for the full year.

Years later, during the 1980s, when my generation of officers led the Army, they placed emphasis on the importance of the length of a command assignment, even in peacetime. The peacetime command tour of duty was two to three years. That policy improved the readiness of the Army and paid dividends in Operation Desert Storm, rebuilding the reputation of the Army as a first class fighting unit.

VICIOUS STORM

Colonel Graves Vung Tau meeting ended around noon on Sunday. I stayed on long enough to attend the chapel services conducted by Chaplain Einertson, the Group Chaplain. I prayed for God's help to lead my men, for my family, and a just end to the war. Einertson was an extraordinary chaplain and, many years later he became a Major General and the Chief of Chaplains of the Army.

I left Vung Tau and flew to several work sites to check on progress and to talk with the officers and men about their work and problems. The heavy rains were crippling their efforts.

When my chopper tried to approach Camp Viking late that day we ran into a vicious storm that rocked the Huey. The pilot tried to fly into the storm and over the storm but after one-half hour of very turbulent weather it was obvious that the danger was too great to continue to Camp Viking. The pilot flew back to Vung Tau. I did not like being absent from the battalion for two nights. Paul Fleri gave me an update over the radio about events at my CP. All was well, but very wet. The next day the only way that I could get back to Camp Viking was to fly to Long Binh in a fixed wing plane, where I was able to catch a chopper flying to Dong Tam. Williams met me in Dong Tam and drove me back to Camp Viking. The lack of a dedicated chopper resulted in a lost day.

*****

By mid-October the rains were so intense that they seemed to have won the battle. They usually started around 17:30 hours and continued all night. Many days passed without sunshine. The silty clay soil was saturated and there was little sunlight to dry out the road surfaces. Some of our jobs had come to a virtual standstill. Earthwork construction was halted because operating the equipment caused more damage than good. However, the two companies in Dong Tam were able to continue working without a halt and the men made excellent progress.

SOME PERSONAL OBSERVATIONS

Letters from home were very important to the soldiers' morale, but the mail was very slow. It took about eight to ten days for a letter to travel from Libby in Virginia to me in Vietnam. When I received her first letter, it seemed like I had been away from home for months and rejoiced that my family was doing well. She usually wrote every day, but several days would pass with no letter and then three or four letters would arrive in the same delivery. It was difficult to carry on a discussion or to get answers to questions, due to the length of time to send and then receive a letter.

After several months, we invested in a couple of tape recorders, to record our conversations; however, tapes took as long as letters. It was great to hear the voices of my wife, daughter, and son. I regret that we did not save the tapes. Fortunately, we continued to write letters and my wife saved them; they have been invaluable in recalling many details about that year in Vietnam. As I write this narrative, I realize that the written word is the best source of information about our past lives. I tried to write to my family every night, but my days and nights were so busy that I did not meet that goal many times. It was usually about mid-night by the time I was able to finish my duties and write a letter.

My wife, like the wives of all servicemen serving overseas, was responsible for our family. She had two children to love and care for, and she worked a full eight-hour day at the Bank of Alexandria. She began working there about two years before I left for Vietnam because my Army pay was not adequate to sustain our needs. We had a mortgage to pay and we planned to send our two teenagers to college; we had to save for their tuition. My busy life in Vietnam left little time to worry about my family, but I knew that Libby was doing an outstanding job in my absence. She always managed very well. Even when I was home, I worked long hours, so she had the responsibility of managing the family.

I adjusted to the heat and humidity. The daily rainstorms soaked me to the skin, but it dried, and it was not long before I was soaking wet with sweat from the humidity. The Vietnam era "flak" vests were hot and uncomfortable but a necessary item. I sat on my vest when I flew in helicopters to protect my fanny from small arms fire. A Viet Cong bullet killed an engineer battalion commander that way. Mosquitoes and bugs were so plentiful that I used bug spray like after-shave lotion. The daily malaria pills did not seem to bother me.

Regarding sanitation, cut down 55-gallon drums with wooden seat covers served as our latrines. They were "flushed" every day when soaked with diesel fuel and then burned. The black oily smoke and stench is memorable.

A Military Affiliated Radio Service (MARS) radio equipped truck came to Camp Viking twice. MARS enabled a soldier to speak with his family back in CONUS. Our men lined up anxiously waiting their turn to talk with their families. When my turn came, it was a delight to hear their voices and to know that everything was all right at home. The bad part of the call was that it reminded me how much I missed my wife and children. Today, soldiers can talk with and see their families on Skype, and Face Time.

COLONEL PARFITT

Before General Chapman relinquished command and left for a new assignment, he visited Camp Viking to thank me, and my men for their dedicated service. After a lengthy discussion in my office, we walked to the mess tent and ate lunch with the troops. I would miss his leadership. After serving in Vietnam, he was promoted to Major General and commanded the Pacific Ocean Division of the Corps of Engineers in Hawaii. Later, he served in the Office of the Chief of Engineers, as Deputy Commanding General of the Army's Combat Development Command, and with the Office of the Secretary of Defense.

Colonel Harold R. Parfitt assumed command of the 20th Brigade. He was on the promotion list to be a Brigadier General. He graduated from West Point during WWII in 1943, served in a combat engineer battalion in Europe during WWII, and received wounds during that operation. During the Korean War, he commanded a combat engineer battalion. Later, he served on the staff and faculty of the Engineer School at Fort Belvoir, as the District Engineer for the Jacksonville, Florida District, and, just prior to his Vietnam assignment, he had been the Lieutenant Governor of the Panama Canal Company.

During his first visit, on Wednesday, 6 November, the battalion staff presented a series of briefings to familiarize him with our operations. I told him about our maintenance and supply problems and the actions we were taking to correct them. As with Colonel Graves, I did not want him to learn of my problems from other sources. After the briefings, I walked him around Camp Viking to see our living and working facilities and our defensive positions.

I got off to a poor start with my new Brigade commander when we flew to Dong Tam. As Murphy's Law would dictate, the construction project was not up to my expectations. Colonel Parfitt was not initially impressed with the battalion. At Ben Luc firebase, a heavy rain had flooded a section of the rebuilt roads. At Can Giuoc firebase, work has stopped on the bunkers because the bridge timbers, needed for the construction, had not been delivered.

Colonel Graves and Colonel Parfitt never seemed satisfied with the battalion; however, he did not offer strong criticisms. Although every project was on schedule, pressure from the chain of command was more intense than ever before. Sometimes, I thought that they were comparing my combat battalion with the construction battalions that worked on easier to understand construction projects; ours were so diverse and performed primarily by platoons, except for the Dong Tam work. I was a little discouraged, but I knew that my officers and men performed their duties under extremely difficult conditions above and beyond the call of duty. I did my best to be more open with my officers and men by offering praise for their good work and corrections when needed.

*****

One day, Colonel Graves and I spent an hour in my CP reviewing the battalion's commitments and operations. I discussed both the good news and the not so good news. At that time, elements of the battalion performed directed missions at many distant locations in Long An Province and the Mekong Delta, so command and control of was a challenge for me. Communications with the outlying units was difficult. The simple act of supplying and supporting our dispersed units was challenging. I wanted Colonel Graves to understand how and where the battalion ran and what we were doing about our difficulties. The better I kept him informed, the better decisions he could make about the battalion. Following our meeting, we embarked on a routine inspection of operations.

PRESIDENTIAL ELECTIONS AND THE WAR

Prior to my arrival in Vietnam, President Lyndon B. Johnson had halted bombing operations over the northern portion of the North Vietnam in order to encourage Hanoi to begin peace negotiations. Hanoi agreed to discuss a bombing halt, and both parties met in Paris in May 1968, but there was no progress because the North Vietnamese negotiators demanded that all bombing of North Vietnam end.

On 31 October 1968, President Johnson agreed to end all air strikes and new negotiations began. However, President Johnson's halt to the bombing of North Vietnam did not stop North Vietnam's efforts to increase the tempo of the war in the Delta. I believe the President's decision allowed the North Vietnamese to increase its supply of men, supplies, weapons, and ammunition to units in the south resulting in more casualties in my battalion as they increased the intensity of the attacks.

That was their answer to the unilateral decision.

My primary sources of news were the Pacific Stars and Stripes, the Armed Forces Radio, and letters from home. Never once did I read about successful results in the Mekong Delta. The war correspondents preferred to write about the battles in the highlands and along the DMZ, that was big news. Rocket attacks in Danang and Saigon were big news, but those correspondents did not come south of Saigon to report on the success of the pacification program and the progress that the 9th Division had made in denying so many sanctuaries from the Viet Cong.

To those of us in the Delta, the war was very real. Soldiers died every day as the Viet Cong attacked with rockets, mortars, RPGs, machine guns, snipers, grenades, and other weapons that North Vietnam supplied down the Ho Chi Minh Trail. It was a terrible mistake to not cut off the Ho Chi Minh Trail. That was a political decision. If we are to fight, we must fight to win.

Although the TET offensive in January 1968 resulted in a defeat of the Viet Cong and North Vietnamese Army Forces, the anti-war news media used news of TET to imply that it had been a defeat of our forces to further undermine public support for continuing the war. Back in the US, the riots in the streets and on the campuses, would eventually cause the US to withdraw from the fight.

Senator Hubert Humphrey and Richard Nixon were candidates for president and they pandered to the growing number of anti-war protesters. Senator Hubert Humphrey said that he would remove all US troops from Vietnam by the end of 1969, a clear declaration that he had no intent to win the war. His opponent Richard Nixon also promised to end the war and win the peace with "honor," but without winning.

The politicians' talk about a unilateral withdrawal encouraged the Viet Cong and the North Vietnamese to increase their attacks so the anti-war movement in the United States would place more pressure on President Johnson to end the war.

Tuesday, 5 November 1968, was Election Day back in the United States. On 8 November, we heard that Richard Nixon had won the election. I wondered what that would mean to us in Vietnam. Working at the battalion level I did not realize that our politicians had already given up any hope of winning the war. I and my soldiers put their lives at risk every day while our diplomats and politicians negotiated a retreat. The North Vietnamese won the negotiations because the United States had already shown that we were going to withdraw and turn the war over to the South Vietnamese.

The enemy's strategy wore down the American people's will to continue the war and our political leaders finally decide that the price of the war was too high, and the US would withdraw our forces. It was tragic that they took so long to make that decision. Our soldiers paid a terrible price. It was particularly irksome for me to hear Senator Ted Kennedy speak against the war since his brother, JFK, was the President who made the original mistake to escalate US involvement in Vietnam without considering the consequences.

In my military mind, I learned that if you do not win, you lose. Like it or not, a professional officer and soldier I was duty bound to obey orders from my chain of command. I had enough to worry about within my sphere of influence. I performed my mission to the very best of my ability.

DONG TAM WORK

I was encouraged during my inspection trips in Dong Tam as Bravo and Delta companies were on schedule and their work was very good. Under Bill Garcia's leadership, they had concentrated on the high priority facilities. I had not forgotten General Ewell's demand that we finish on schedule. The first task scheduled for completion was the division's laundry.

I inspected several vehicles and decided that the equipment operators were doing a better job taking care of their equipment. Also, the companies were correcting their supply records. I was pleased to see the positive action by the two company commanders and their men.

FRIENDLY FIRE

Early one morning, at 04:15 hours, we had a rude awakening. Several mortar rounds landed within the compound causing one death and two wounded. We went on red alert and the men raced from their bunks to their fighting positions, prepared to repulse a ground attack in the early morning

Figure 45 Dong Tam laundry, constructed by the 86th Combat Engineers

rain. We waited for an attack, but it did not come. Later that day, I was devastated to learn that a 9th Division unit had fired the incoming rounds. It was a friendly fire tragedy caused by an infantry unit that was patrolling off to our north. When they contacted a North Vietnamese Army unit they called for mortar support. Either they gave the wrong coordinates for the North Vietnamese Army location, or their gunners missed their aim. Artillery from Dong Tam never caused friendly fire casualties.

*****

Around 2 AM one night an alert guard stationed on the outer perimeter called the CP to report strange movements about two hundred yards in front of his position. Was it the beginning of a sneak attack The CP flashed the news within the base and alerted all the men. I dashed up the guard tower to see what I could see through a night vision scope. No movement was visible. I was one step short of sending the men to their defensive fighting positions when I dispatched a non-commissioned officer, armed with a night vision scope, to the perimeter to talk with the guard that reported the incident. The guard pointed in the direction of the noise and when the non-commissioned officer looked through the night vision device he saw several water buffalos grazing in the rice paddies between Camp Viking and the Binh Duc airstrip.

OFFICERS= CLUB

The Officer's Club at Viking was a tent structure like the rest of the hooches. While it was not worthy of the name, it was a place where the officers could relax and have a beer. The non-commissioned officers and the enlisted men occupied a larger tent. Occasionally the officers met for a beer, a steak, or a pizza. The consumption of beer was moderate. Alcoholism was not a problem. Conversation was usually about operations, but there were some good war stories and a few good jokes. When my chopper crashed on Friday the 13th I had left my flak vest on the damaged Huey. One evening at the club, the headquarters company commander presented me with a new vest, and inscribed on the back was, *what me worry?*

595 LIGHT EQUIPMENT COMPANY CHANGE OF COMMAND

The 595 Light Equipment Company was in good condition when Captain Zang's Vietnam tour was over, and he was ready for leave for CONUS. At his change of command formation at Bear Cat, I received the 595th Company's guidon from Captain Zang and handed it to First Lieutenant Yancey Jones, the new commander of the 595 Light Equipment Company. During the brief ceremony, I commended the soldiers and officers for their work and presented purple hearts to Staff Sergeant George M. Rutter and Specialist Four Gary P. Small.

I selected Jones for the job because he had performed brilliantly as Bill Garcia's Assistant Operations Officer. What he may have lacked in command experience he made up for in his authenticity and his natural leadership qualities. I believed that Jones was the right man, and over the next few months, my judgment of Jones proved to be correct. He was an outstanding company commander. To ensure success I assigned a few of the best incoming non-commissioned officers to the company. Under his command, his company was a source of strength for the battalion.

A MURDER

There was one case of murder in the battalion, a tragic situation in the 595 Light Equipment Company that occurred shortly after Lieutenant Jones assumed command. When an incident like that occurred, I wondered what was coming at us next.

A Hispanic soldier and an African American soldier had a

Figure 46 Change of command 595 Light Equipment Company

fight, and the Hispanic used his rifle to settle the argument by shooting the other man in the face. It was tragic. No one knew what the fight was about. The next morning, Chaplain Mills and I flew to Bear Cat to hold a memorial service for the murdered soldier.

I ordered the company commander, Lieutenant Jones, to conduct a preliminary investigation with the help of two officers from the battalion staff. Jones' investigation revealed little information about the disagreement and that drugs and alcohol were not involved.

Next, I assigned Major Garcia to conduct a formal investigation according to the Army Regulations and the Uniform Code of Military Justice. The investigation conflicted with important work in his Operations Office, but the investigation was a top priority issue. The investigation concluded that the Hispanic soldier did kill the African American. Based on those findings I arranged for a Court Martial trial, which found the accused guilty of murder. We turned him over to the Military Police and that is the last I knew of the incident.

HEADQUARTERS COMPANY CHANGE OF COMMAND

The Headquarters Company Commander, Captain Marion M. Meeks, completed his Vietnam tour. He had been an excellent leader of his company, a challenge for a headquarters unit. At his change-of-command ceremony, I took the company guidon from Meeks and passed it to First Lieutenant Lee Berglund who had been the company executive officer. He was well qualified and was familiar with the unique mission of the company.

The day before Captain Meeks was due to leave, I learned that he had not completed the inventory and Lieutenant Berglund would not sign for the property. I refused to release Meeks and required that he stay on for several more days until the inventory was competed. There seemed to be a myth that there was no need to worry about equipment accountability. That was not true in my battalion.

*****

I attended a meeting at the 9th Division Headquarters with Major General Ewell, Brigadier General Timothy, and Colonel Graves to review the construction program and to prepare plans to support the division during the dry season. Others at the meeting were Guy Jester and Ralph Sievers, commander of the 93rd Construction Battalion.

*****

The weather turned vicious. Heavy rains accompanied by extremely high winds tore the roofs off many of the Viking hooches.

*****

Late in November, the battalion Surgeon, Captain E. G. Vega left for reassignment in CONUS. His replacement was Captain Robert Falkner. Both medics were superior doctors and good officers.

CHAPLAIN MILLS

Soldiers in combat must have access to spiritual leaders, because that old story that soldiers turn to God in combat is not a myth. Chaplain Harold Mills was a Baptist and I am an Episcopalian, both devout Christians. Together

Figure 47 Chaplain Mills conducted services on the construction sites.

we attended and grieved at too many grief-stricken memorial services to honor our fallen engineers. He was a spiritual leader for me and for the men; he brought God's word and comfort to the men when he visited with them in the field, and when he offered individual counseling. He travelled with me often to visit our men in far-flung units and to conduct non-denominational services for them. He used the hood of a jeep, the side of a crane, or whatever else was convenient, to set up an altar on which he placed a cross. Men gathered around him for prayers, bible readings, singing, and communion. On a few rare occasions, a Roman Catholic chaplain served our men. There were no Jewish chaplains available. Chaplains are an essential part of our Army. Some politically correct citizens have tried to do away with chaplains in the military. That would be a terrible step to undermine the strength of the American soldier.

Chaplain Mills had no trouble convincing me that we needed a chapel at Camp Viking. It was a sanctuary for all of us. The chapel was a physical symbol of our faith. We held a special service to dedicate the battalion's chapel. Chaplain Mills and Chaplain Norris L. Einertson, the Group Chaplain, led the service.

Volunteers built the chapel with a wood floor and a frame for the chapel tent. They made a crude altar table to hold a cross. He borrowed folding chairs from the mess hall each Sunday for services. Many of our men at Camp Viking attended chapel on Sundays. Chaplain Mills used the tent during the week to meet with men who needed counseling.

AWARDS

On three occasions, I assembled the company commanders, their First Sergeants, and guidon bearers at Camp Viking to honor our engineer soldiers for their distinguished and heroic performance of duty. It was important to recognize their work and courage. I presented many Bronze Star Medals, Commendation Medals, and too many Purple Hearts.

Figure 48 Awards ceremony
at Camp Viking

In the tradition of WWII and Korea, our young engineers proudly served their country, did their duty, and performed dangerous work. I will always have a high regard for their courage. They put their lives on the line every day, doing their duty.

I recommended awards for many of our courageous engineers; however, the 20th Brigade's policy was very conservative, and too many

of my recommendations were denied, so many of my young officers and enlisted men went home with no recognition of their contribution to the Vietnam War. Most all those brave 5-ton truck drivers deserved, at the least, a Commendation Medal. Somehow the personnel people at 20th Brigade Headquarters, isolated from the combat area, could not visualize truck drivers as brave soldiers. General Ewell's policy for awards in the 9th Division seemed to be too liberal. I was told that every one of his soldiers must return to CONUS with at least one decoration.

Figure 49 LTC presents medals

General Parker flew to Camp Viking on one of those occasions to present the Silver Star for Gallantry in Action to Specialist Five Robert L. Coon of Headquarters Company while he was assigned to the Land Clearing Team. As mentioned previously, during a Viet Cong attack, a mortar round hit the ammunition bunker and it burst into flames. Specialist Coon ran from his protected position, through a hail of enemy shrapnel and small arms fire, to a nearby bulldozer. He drove the dozer to the bunker and covered the bunker with earth to smother the fire.

Figure 50 General Parker present Legion of Merit to LTC Peixotto

General Parker awarded other Bronze Star Medals and Commendation Medals to many other deserving engineers and the Legion of Merit to LTC Peixotto.

SERGEANT MAJOR MEEKER DEPARTS

It was a sad day for me when Sergeant Major Meeker left the battalion. The night before he left, Paul Fleri, Bill Garcia, and I treated him to a bottle of champagne and an evening of pure camaraderie. I have no idea where the champagne came from, but Paul had a lot of initiative. The next day I took Meeker to Long Binh in my chopper where he was to out-process. It was difficult for me to say goodbye to that magnificent soldier. I owe so much to him. He was very

Figure 51 SGM McCurley

helpful to me as I took over the command of the battalion. The men of the battalion also owe a lot to him because of the way he had looked out for their interests. I recommended that he be awarded the Legion of Merit, but my recommendation was disapproved at higher headquarters. He received the Bronze Star Medal.

*****

Three weeks later, Sergeant Major John McCurley was assigned to the battalion. He was another fine soldier and we worked together in the same manner that Meeker had done.

*****

I flew from Long Binh to Dong Tam to attend a meeting with members of the division staff and Lieutenant Colonel Jester to confer about the division's current and future construction programs. Before heading back to Camp

Figure 52 Dong Tam Aviation Operations Building Viking, I promoted Bravo Company's commander, Lieutenant Robinson, to Captain.

When I returned to Camp Viking that night, there were several letters from my family on my desk, but I could not read them until late that night after working with Paul Fleri, Bill Garcia, and the staff. There is no substitute for a letter from your loved ones to lift your morale. Libby's and Vivian's letters were filled with news of their busy lives, and Ernest sent a tape with the music from the movie Dr. Zhivago, one of my favorites. The music sounded great to my ears after the steady playing of popular music on the Armed Forces Radio.

DONG TAM CONSTRUCTION WINDS DOWN

The battalion's construction program in Dong Tam was nearing a successful completion, thanks to the excellent work of the men in both companies, and Bill Garcia's planning and leadership. It was the largest single effort of the battalion and a high priority for the 9th Division.

The division's laundry was the first project completed. It had been a difficult job because the work involved carpentry, plumbing, and electrical installations; however, our engineers had been trained as combat engineers, not as construction engineers like those in the construction battalions. Our men learned enough skills on the job and completed the laundry on time. The quality of their work was good.

Figure 53 Dong Tam Maintenance Facilities

I attended a simple ribbon cutting ceremony for the laundry; the 9th Division Band played music for the ceremony. I commended the men and said that building a laundry may not be too exciting, but some fifteen thousand soldiers needed some clean jungle fatigues after slogging around in the rice paddies. It was a laundry the men could be proud of, but certainly not a typical project for combat engineers. I was very pleased that they completed the job on schedule.

Next, Bravo Company constructed the 14,000 square foot aviation operations building and four 12,000 square foot vehicle maintenance buildings. They also worked on the roads, revetments, six head-walls and several ditches.

Through the outstanding drive, dedication and leadership at the company and platoon level, they completed all the facilities in advance of the scheduled dates. I commended the men for an excellent job.

While Lieutenant Robinson had a bad start, he turned the job around and earned my strongest accolades. The company prepared for the next mission.

DELTA COMPANY CHANGE OF COMMAND

When it came time for Captain Joseph G. Huber, Jr. to leave, I officiated at a change of command ceremony in Dong Tam where Captain Andy Dykes assumed command of the company. Dykes, a West Point graduate, had recently arrived and was well qualified to take command of a company.

RELIABLE ACADEMY

Delta Company's construction of Reliable Non-Commissioned Officers Academy was another high priority project for General Ewell, because the division needed the facility to train new non-commissioned officers.

Before vertical construction began, the 595th Company's earthmovers transported fill material to raise the foundation level for nine buildings by more than two and one-half feet. While the earthwork was underway, hampered by the heavy rains, the battalion's S-4 stockpiled the construction material at the work site.

Once they completed the earthwork, the men mixed batches of concrete to construct nine 20 by 100-foot concrete building slabs. When they completed the foundations, they constructed eight two-story wood barracks and a classroom building.

Delta Company completed the Academy in November ahead of the deadline for the project, surprising the sidewalk-supervisors and General Ewell. At the turnover ceremony in late November 1968, Captain Dykes, presented the Assistant Division Commander, Brigadier General Gunn, a pair of scissors to cut the ribbon. A very pleased General Ewell commended the battalion for the excellent work.

*****

A typhoon passed through our area and deposited eight inches of rain. The next morning Camp Viking was a lake. All vehicles stayed in place until the soil became passable. The dry season was yet to come; however, we were already preparing plans for important projects when it arrived.

*****

One night in November the several mortar rounds landed in Camp Viking, but our infantrymen used our mortars to counter their fire when I saw the flashes from their mortars. Next, the Dusters fired in the area, ending the attack. We suffered no casualties.

That same night, the Viet Cong attacked Vung Tau with twenty rockets. Colonel Graves reported that there were no hits on the 34th Group compound. The VC repeated their attack on us the next night.

*****

Intensive fighting broke out once again to the north of Camp Viking when a 7th Division ARVN unit tangled with a large North Vietnam Army unit. We went on red alert and manned all fighting positions. The fight continued most of the night. At 02:30 hours mortar and rockets began landing inside our perimeter. I was unable to see the source of the mortars and rockets, so I called on the 4.2-inch mortars in Dong Tam to hit several of the pre-designated areas. That ended the VC's attacks. By morning the situation had quieted down, but the men had not gotten much rest during the night. Once again, I thanked God that we suffered no casualties. One of the blessings, if there were any in that war, was that the North Vietnam Army and Viet Cong were not well trained, and their aim was poor.

CAO LANH OPERATION

General Ewell planned to increase offensive operations in Ding Tuong Province and eventually move a brigade into the western Mekong Delta during the dry season to attack the enemy near the Cambodian border and cut off their supplies, weapons, ammunition, and troops that continued to flow down the Ho Chi Minh Trail. Ewell's plans involved the 34th Group, the 9th Division, Special Forces, and the Vietnamese 44th Special Tactical Zone.

I thought that we should have gone into Cambodia and Laos to attack their bases, but our political leaders, the media, and the anti-war crowd opposed any offensive act outside of Vietnam. Yes, such an offensive would have violated the sanctity of Cambodia, but I believe that the lives of young American soldiers should have been more important. Once again, it was obvious that President Johnson and the Washington "experts' were not planning to win the war.

Ewell's plan to attack the enemy in the western area of the Mekong Delta depended on the construction of a new base and an airfield near the town of Cao Lanh. Ewell tasked the 34th Group to construct that base, so naturally Colonel Graves assigned the job to the 86th Engineers. As was always the case, General Ewell was anxious to complete construction to start operations when the dry season began. In the meantime, my men would be working in the mud.

Requirements for the new base included a runway surfaced with M8-A1 steel landing mats, two turn around areas, a taxiway, a parking apron, four helicopter pads with protective revetments, several large POL storage tanks, four helicopter rearmament pads, an ammunition storage area, eight refueling pads with protective revetments, and an eight-foot high earth berm around the perimeter of the area to protect the facilities from direct-fire weapons. Fighting bunkers and watchtowers on the berm would defend the perimeter of the base.

Figure 54 An ARVN artillery unit provided fire support at Cao Lanh construction base for Bravo Company.

A dredge had already pumped half a million cubic meters of silty-clay from the bottom of the Mekong River onto the area, in the same manner they prepared for the construction of Dong Tam.

I assigned that company-sized project to Captain Robinson's Bravo Company, as he and his engineers were finishing the construction work in Dong Tam.

I met with Captain Robinson, Bill Garcia, Captain Ajer, and officers from the 9th Division staff to develop plans for the operation, to estimate the amount of supplies and construction material Bravo Company needed for the project, and to move the company and supplies up the

Mekong River to the Cao Lanh construction site. Supplies for the operation included hundreds of bundles of M8-A1 steel landing mat, massive quantities of T-17 membrane, and thousands of bags of cement.

As they continued to develop the plans, I made the first of many long flights up the Mekong River to Cao Lanh to reconnoiter the construction area and coordinate our work with local US, and Vietnamese authorities.

My chopper landed in downtown Cao Lanh on a small chopper pad. I talked with the commander of MACV Advisory Team 50 about his work with the ARVN units. We met the ARVN commander who told me about how limited his units were in blocking large North Vietnamese Army units entering the area, but he would do what he could to help Bravo Company with security, because there were no U.S. Army combat units in the area. We arranged to coordinate artillery fire support from an ARVN 105-mm artillery battery. I also paid a courtesy call on the Province Chief.

I talked with the leader of a Special Forces Team about his operations along the Cambodian border to interdict traffic coming down the Ho Chi Minh Trail. Another small unit, the 52nd Signal Group, was also in Cao Lanh. I believe that unit was an intelligence unit. All three, unit commanders asked me for construction materials to improve their meager living facilities. I assured them that we would help them as much as possible.

Before I left Cao Lanh, I looked over the large area that the dredge had created. The dredged material was slowly draining and very muddy. Earth moving would be sloppy and difficult. Bravo Company first task would be to set up its own base and develop a good defensive plan and perimeter.

By mid-November, a fleet of Navy landing craft had assembled in Dong Tam's harbor to move Bravo Company, its supplies, and construction materials up the Mekong River. Plans were set to ship routine resupplies up Mekong River from Dong Tam. CH-47 cargo helicopters would transport rations, mail, ammunition, some POL, and emergency supplies.

A "fleet" of loaded landing craft sailed out of the little port in Dong Tam on 20 November 1968 and it took the best part of one day to travel up the river. The landing craft arrived at the objective area just before nightfall; however, the men stayed on the landing craft overnight because it was too risky to set up a camp in the dark. At first light, Bravo Company's engineers unloaded the landing craft and moved, in full force, to the construction site. Before the sun had set that day, they had set up tents, other basic facilities, and set up an initial perimeter defensive system. During the next few days they completed constructing the base camp and defensive system. Bravo Company's men had not been engaged in combat situations while they worked in Dong Tam; however, at Cao Lanh they were isolated and would need to defend themselves.

Their security situation was a challenge. Bravo Company fought several battles with the Viet Cong. One dark night late in February, the Viet Cong tried to break through the security perimeter and enter the company's compound, but they set off trip flares in the barbed wire. Bravo Company's guards alerted the rest of the company and they quickly manned fighting positions on the perimeter of the compound. The Viet Cong attacked for fifteen minutes with intense automatic weapons fire and with more than twenty mortar rounds. The engineers laid down a withering fire and the Viet Cong retreated. Thankfully our men suffered no casualties. That was not true during other attacks, there were casualties and Medevac choppers took the wounded men to the hospital at Dong Tam.

Figure 55 A CH-47 Chinook dropping supplies

I was dependent on the battalion's radios to communicate with all my company commanders; however, the radios used by the battalion were unable to communicate directly with Captain Robinson and Bravo Company because Cao Lanh more than sixty miles from Camp Viking and that exceeded the range of our radios. Our communications officer worked with the 9th Division's Signal battalion and they gave us a set of long range radios that could reach Cao Lanh, so we were in constant contact with all our companies.

The earth moving operations were difficult, because water still saturated the silty-clay dredged material. Captain Robinson and his engineers did the best they could under the circumstances while the monsoon rains continued. The use of granular material in the western Delta was out of the question; there was none. Our rock and laterite supplies were too far away. While the work area dried, the men stockpiled construction material, and developed the company's base.

The day before Thanksgiving, Sergeant Major McCurley, Chaplain Mills, and I flew to Cao Lanh to deliver a hot turkey dinner and the  mail. Our Huey was so heavily loaded that it had difficultly lifting off the pad at Viking. The men at Cao Lanh were not always glad to see the Colonel, but they were that day as they ate a hot turkey dinner.

Figure 56 LTC Peixotto talks with men in Bravo Company, Thanksgiving

Captain Robinson's officers and non-commissioned officers were doing well under very challenging circumstances. The men's morale was good, and danger from the Viet Cong did not dampen their spirits. Sergeant Major McCurley and I were satisfied with their progress; however, I worried because the mission would be difficult to complete on schedule. Although the wet condition of the soil was difficult to manage, the company made limited progress with their dozers, front loaders, and 5-ton trucks.

I found it necessary to fly to Cao Lanh every other day because of my concern for the men and the challenging mission to turn a water soaked dredged soil into a workable base. The trip took the better part of the day and limited my ability to inspect the many other projects.

THANKSGIVING

Thanksgiving Day was cold and dreary. Chaplain Mills conducted Thanksgiving services in our chapel. I read from the Bible and lead a prayer of thanksgiving. We were thankful for God's bounty and his love. We prayed for safe deliverance.

I had planned to miss Thanksgiving dinner at Camp Viking to visit all my companies and talk with as many of the officers and men as possible. However, my plans changed when Colonel Graves announced that he wanted to visit Bravo Company and inspect conditions at the Cao Lanh construction site. He picked me up at the Camp Viking helipad and we flew west for about fifty miles until we met the front of a very violent storm. As our pilot tried to fly through and over the storm the visibility decreased rapidly, and the winds were so turbulent that the Huey seemed uncontrollable at times. When it became too perilous to continue flying west, we had no other choice than to turn back, flying, at full speed, just in front of the leading edge of the storm. The last thing Graves and I wanted to do was to go down in the middle of the Plain of Reeds. Engulfed by the storm, by God's grace, we made it back to Dong Tam, ending another memorable "white knuckles" flight.

Ralph Sievers met us at the heliport and invited us and the chopper crew to join his battalion's Thanksgiving dinner. The Army spared nothing for the troops on Thanksgiving. I will always wonder how so many turkeys, sweet potatoes, cans of cranberry sauce, and so on could make it through the supply system when that same system could not supply essential repair parts. After dinner Colonel Graves and I had a lengthy one-on-one discussion about the battalion's operations and problems. He left for Vung Tau when the storm had passed.

I then visited Delta Company as they were finishing their Thanksgiving Dinner. I ate lightly and enjoyed being with the men and talked with Captain Dykes about a pending mission for his company in eastern Long An Province.

After the worst part of the storm passed on to the east, I was able to drive to Camp Viking in a borrowed jeep. It was still raining, and the rain soak me to the skin, but that was not at all unusual. Friday morning the typhoon moved on to the east, leaving another sea of mud.

A DAY WITH MAJOR GENERAL PARKER

I met General Parker early one morning at the Tan An bridge to look over the work as the men were driving more piles and placing cyclone fencing around the piers. He was pleased with the progress and commended Captain Cidras and his men.

We flew to Cao Lanh for his first inspection of that project. Work on the airfield was progressing as well as possible despite the saturated dredged material. The quality of the work was as good as it could be under the adverse circumstances. General Parker left me at Cao Lanh. I made a thorough inspection of the work and checked on the security plans before returning to Camp Viking late that afternoon.

*****

Late in December, the Colonel Graves told me to accelerate work on the Cao Lanh airfield, because the 9th Division was eager to move units to the new base. Although I had been up most of the night, due to enemy action, I was off, early in the morning, on another flight to Cao Lanh. I walked over the entire project to examine the progress and discuss the work with Captain Robinson and his non-commissioned officers. I studied their maintenance records to ensure that the men were taking care of their equipment and that they received needed logistic support from the battalion. The project was on schedule and the men were doing a decent job, considering the lousy conditions.

I reviewed the work schedule with Captain Robinson and we examined alternatives to speed up the operation. There was very little slack in the schedule. I had no other resources within the battalion to reinforce the company and speed up the work. I concluded that I could not accelerate the schedule, regardless of the 34th Group's order. On my return to Viking, I told Colonel Graves that I could not accelerate the work, but Bravo Company would finish the work on schedule. He did not like my answer, but he accepted my evaluation of the situation.

UPDATES FOR GENERAL EWELL

Whenever possible, I went to Dong Tam late in the afternoon to attend the evening update for General Ewell. The staff presented the latest information about the enemy strength and movement, results of combat actions, plans for future combat actions, logistics, personnel, and all the other details involved in running a large organization engaged in combat. Those briefings were my primary source of information about friendly and enemy operations in our area. After the update one evening, General Gunn, the Assistant Division Commander, invited me to stay and attend dinner in the General Officers Mess, a very nice treat. After supper, a slick (stripped Huey) picked me up at the chopper pad in Dong Tam for a short night-flight back to Camp Viking.

Late in December, the three engineer battalions that supported the 9th Division received special commendations at a small ceremony in my CP. Brigadier General Frank Gunn awarded the Bronze Star Medal to LTC Guy Jester, 15th Engineers, LTC Ralph Sievers, 93rd Engineers, and me, LTC Peixotto. The cooperation and close coordination among the three battalions had been excellent. Like all awards presented to commanders, the Bronze Star Medal that I received was a tribute to the demanding work and courage of the men in my battalion. The award came as a very pleasant surprise.

595 LIGHT EQUIPMENT COMPANY TO VIKING

When the 595 Light Equipment Company's CP moved from Bear Cat to Camp Viking in December, I tasked Lieutenant Jones to construct a new road on the north side of the camp to connect Camp Viking directly to highway QL-4. The only entry to Camp Viking was to cross the Bailey Bridge and drive through My Tho. The 2nd Platoon led by First Lieutenant Stephen N. Dettor and Sergeant First Class George G. Whitley constructed the road in 15 days, using large earth moving machines, 290Ms, to move 12,000 cubic yards of fill material. They used Peneprime, a liquid asphalt-oil mixture, to seal the surface of the access road to reduce the dust from truck traffic. The 3rd Platoon, under the leadership of First Lieutenant James E. Jones, and Staff Sergeant Rodney McGorley, upgraded and widened TL-25, between My Tho, Camp Viking, and Dong Tam. That road was the only road into Dong Tam from QL-4.

A NEW MISSION IN LONG AN PROVINCE

I attended a meeting with Major General Ewell, Brigadier General Timothy, and Colonel Graves to learn about General Ewell's plan to commit the 2nd Battalion of the 47th Mechanized Infantry Regiment (2nd /47th Infantry) and a reinforced combat engineer company from my battalion. The 2nd /47th Infantry battalion was the only mechanized infantry battalion in the 9th Division,

The 9th Division's aggressive combat operations had gradually fashioned a reliable military presence in large sections of Long An Province. To gain further access into Viet Cong controlled regions and let more farmers return to their villages, the 9th Division planned a new offensive to extend control over more territory in Long An Province and to pacify Go Cong Province where some strong Viet Cong and North Vietnamese Army units occupied the villages and

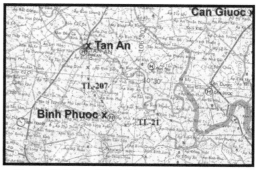

Figure 57 Map of Binh Phuoc area of operations

hidden sanctuaries. They were a threat to Saigon, Tan An, Ben Luc, QL-4, and My Tho.

I committed Captain Dykes and his Delta Company to support the 2nd /47th Infantry during that new offensive operation. It was my only company available once it completed work on the Reliable Academy in Dong Tam. Alpha Company, based at Camp Viking, was engaged in several important projects. Bravo Company was already working at Cao Lanh and would not be available for a couple of months. Charlie Company's 3rd Platoon was constructing protective structure around the Tan An Bridge. The 2nd Platoon was committed to the firebase construction, and the 1st Platoon had moved to the Binh Duc airstrip to construct a C-130 capable airfield. The 595 Light Equipment Company's CP was at Camp Viking and its platoons were committed to support missions at several construction sites; Can Giuoc FSB, Ben Luc FSB, the Tan An bridge, and the Long An road projects.

Since the offensive operation involved the pacification program in Long An Province, I met with Colonel Nu, the Province Chief, in his Tan An office. Over a cup of tea, he told me about his plans to free up large areas of his

Figure 59 Captain Dykes, Commanded Delta Company

province and repopulate it with the farmers that had fled. I studied his maps to find out what roads and bridges he wanted rebuilt. I had to see some of those roads, so we drove to Binh Phuoc on Route 207 in his jeep, escorted by several ARVN jeeps because it was hostile territory. The road was in poor condition; it needed a lot of work to make it useable. I examined several demolished bridges on the side roads; they needed replacement. I was unable to look at all the roads that he wanted to reopen because those roads were impassable and led to Viet Cong sanctuaries. We returned to his office in Tan An and agreed on which roads should take our first efforts.

The next day, Bill Garcia and I made an aerial reconnaissance to make some preliminary estimates of the engineer work that the operation would need. We flew along Route 207 from Tan An to Binh Phuoc, and then over Route TL-21 from Binh Phuoc deep into Go Cong Province. As we flew over TL-21 in Go Cong Province, we saw a road that was in very poor condition and the bridges over three small rivers no longer existed. I was pleased to see many rows of large water filled B-52 bomb craters.

Figure 59 Captain Dykes, Commanded Delta Company

The villages in the area were mostly deserted. Occasionally, we saw Vietnamese in the villages and in the rice paddies. Were they friendly or Viet Cong? We came under fire from some of those peaceful looking peasants. The two door gunners opened fire with their M-60 machine guns to subdue the peasants.

The pilot made several low-level passes for us to get a better look at the condition of the roadbeds and the bridge abutments. Some sections of the roads were non-existent. The pilot took us so low that the chopper collected a few limbs from banana trees on the skids. Back at Viking I tasked Bill Garcia's Operation section to begin planning for the Long An Province mission.

The next day, Bill Garcia dispatched a reconnaissance team to collect data about those roads and bridges that were accessible. Their reports included the road conditions, width, materials, bridges, culverts, rivers, bank conditions, and many other engineering factors that we considered as we planned for the resources needed for a construction project.

During the year, the reconnaissance section surveyed the condition of hundreds of kilometers of roads and reported on one hundred eighty bridges. The men traveled in three-quarter ton trucks armed with .50 caliber machine guns. The reconnaissance team drove through some unfriendly territory and needed their own fire power to defend themselves.

Our mission called for a total make-over of Camp Panther, the 2/47th Infantry's base, which was on the outskirts of Binh Phuoc. Simultaneously, the battalion was to secure and upgrade the condition of thirteen miles of Route 207, *Thunder Road*, from Tan and to Binh Phuoc. Once Camp Panther and Route 207 were secure, the mission called for the construction of a new bridge across the Duc River in Binh Phuoc capable of carrying the M-113s. The final phase of the operation was to support combat operations in Go Cong Province and rebuild more than ten miles of TL-21 to include constructing two more bridges on TL-21.

CAMP PANTHER

Early in December, Captain Dykes' Delta Company left Dong Tam in a long convoy, drove up QL-4 to Tan An, and then down *Thunder Road* to Camp Panther.

Dykes concentrated the men's energies on rebuilding Camp Panther, which the division's 15th Engineers had built during the earlier dry season. There were a few fighting bunkers on the perimeter, and no overhead protection for the infantrymen. Corrugated sheet metal covered their billets to keep them dry from the rain, but the sheet metal was more of a danger than a help during a mortar attack. If a mortar round happened to hit a corrugated roof it would detonate on contact and disperse shrapnel downward on the men, causing heavy casualties.

Figure 60 A recon Team at work

107

The Delta engineers constructed thirteen hardened bunkers to protect themselves and the infantrymen from nightly mortar and rocket attacks. The battalion's 5-ton truck drivers transported the timbers and other material from Dong Tam. Once they completed the well-planned bunker project, the engineers improved the infantrymen's living conditions, helped improve the security of the base, and constructed six all-weather firing platforms for the artillery battery inside of Camp Panther. They increased and improved the fighting bunkers on the perimeter of the base. That added protection was a critical factor in the defense of the base during several vicious Viet Cong attacks.

The heavy monsoon rains had turned Camp Panther into a sea of mud. Two enormous mud holes in the middle of the base where almost large enough to swallow an M-113. Delta's engineers, supported by the 595 Light Equipment Company, rebuilt the interior of Camp Panther with thousands of yards of soil from the local vicinity and with laterite and crushed rock delivered from Tan An and Ben Luc by the battalion's fleet of 5-ton trucks, driven by their courageous drivers.

THUNDER ROAD

The only supply route from Tan and to Binh Phuoc was the two lane un-surfaced road, Route 207. It was in poor condition because the M-113 APC's had damaged the road's surface. The infantrymen named Route 207 *Thunder Road* because Viet Cong mines caused many casualties and damaged the M-113 APCs.

Delta Company's engineers reconstructed *Thunder Road* using heavy equipment from the 595 Light Equipment Company to increase its capability to excavate rice paddy silty clay soil for use on the road. The final work on *Thunder Road* was to add thousands of cubic yards of laterite

Figure 61 Clearing mines on Thunder Road

and rock, hauled to the road by our 5-ton truck drivers. Once they finished rebuilding *Thunder Road*, frequent maintenance was necessary to prevent its deterioration.

Delta Company's engineers detected and cleared the Viet Cong placed mines every morning, before the MPs could open the road to traffic. To avoid detection by our mine detectors, the Viet Cong often relied on command-detonated mines, which they made from plastic explosives, buried deep under the shoulder of the road. They attached the mines to a wire that led to a concealed observation post. The enemy waited patiently to detonate the explosives when selected targets passed by the mines. Some explosive charges were so large that they could blow an M-113 into the air and turn it over killing the infantrymen riding in it.

The 2/47th Infantry conducted nighttime ambushes along *Thunder Road* to stop the mining, but the road was too long to defend its full length. Hardly a night passed when the enemy did not mine the road. Keeping that road open to both military and civilian traffic was important.

Clearing the mines along *Thunder Road* was a dangerous operation for the engineers, because one missed mine could cause the loss of life. Someone in the battalion came up with the idea of building a mine-clearing machine like some used during WWII in Europe. I asked Lieutenant Jones if his welders in the 595 Light Equipment Company could fabricate a mine-clearing machine to detonate anti-personnel and anti-tank land mines. His men took about thirty days to fabricate the mine roller. The huge machine consisted of ninety-six 50-pound two-inch thick steel wheels, cut with acetylene torches from steel plates. They mounted the wheels on an axle that was seventeen feet in front of a 290M tractor. When mines detonated under the wheels, there was no damage to the 290M or the operator. The unique machine was unwieldy, but it detonated many mines; however, the engineers followed behind to detect those mines missed by the machine.

NEWS FROM HOME

Mail from my family informed me that TV and newspaper reports declared that the war was over and there was no action occurring in the Delta. The news disturbed me because it was not true. Our battalion suffered more casualties in December than in any previous month.

34TH GROUP MOVED TO BINH THUY

The 34th Group Headquarters moved from Vung Tau to Binh Thuy late in December. The 36th Engineer Construction Battalion moved from Vung Tau to work on QL-4 near Vinh Long. The move brought the Group closer to us, and communications improved. It also brought the Group staff closer to the war since Vung Tau was a remote R&R center.

*****

On the night of December 20th there was an unusually aggressive Viet Cong attack on Camp Viking. The engineers in the fighting bunkers on the perimeter opened fire along with our Dusters and mortars. The Viet Cong gradually withdrew to a wooded area north of Camp Viking where we could not see them, but they continued to fire mortars and rockets at Camp Viking. I called for artillery support and an air strike to end the threat. We suffered several casualties and some equipment damage.

*****

The weather gradually began to improve. The evenings were exceptionally beautiful. The night brought some cooler breezes, cloudless sky, and a welcome full moon. The full moon was not very romantic, but it gave the Viet Cong less chance for a sneak attack.

*****

The maintenance report at the end of December confirmed that the battalion was making progress. The deadline rate for vehicles and engineer equipment had dropped from twenty-five percent to twenty percent. That was an important change in the right direction, but it was not yet satisfactory. A twenty percent deadline rate denied the battalion the use of the needed dozers, trucks etc. The USARV goal was ten percent. The repair parts shortage was still the leading cause for the deadlines. The non-commissioned officer expediter in Long Binh helped to reduce the deadline rate but many parts were not available in Long Binh. That was a poor reflection on the Army's supply system.

The reduction in the deadline rate was good news and a morale booster for the officers, non-commissioned officers, and enlisted men. I reviewed the data for each item of equipment listed in the report to ensure that it was as correct as humanly possible. I did not want to make a false report to cover up our problems. The officers knew that I wanted the correct facts, no matter how bad that might be for the companies and the battalion. I worked late that night with Ed Ajer to correct a few errors in the report.

CHRISTMAS 1968

I will never forget Christmas of 1968. The 9th Division Intelligence section warned that Viet Cong units were assembling in our vicinity and they might attack Camp Viking and My Tho. It was not a holiday for the Viet Cong, so we kept an eye out for them; we would not let them catch us with our guard down.

I ordered all work to cease on Christmas Day, so the men could relax and enjoy the day as much as possible; however, all our guard posts and perimeter positions were on full alert. I wanted to visit all my companies on Christmas day; however, I could not because the 20th Brigade grounded the helicopters for the day, so the pilots and crew to enjoy the day. Chaplain Mills conducted an inspirational Christmas service in our tent-chapel; however, our men in the field had no access to a religious celebration of the birth of Jesus Christ.

Our cooks served a full Christmas dinner in the mess hall: shrimp cocktail, roast turkey, gravy, cornbread dressing, cranberry sauce, mashed potatoes, glazed sweet potatoes, mixed vegetables, relishes, hot rolls with butter, mincemeat pie, pumpkin pie with whipped topping, assorted nuts, candy, fresh fruits, iced tea, and milk. The cooks worked extra hard preparing and serving the meal. The men ate very well. Every soldier received a copy of the menu with a message from General Creighton W. Abrams, which closed with the statement, "As we face the coming New Year, may we each pray for success in our mission, peace on earth, and good will for all mankind.

The company commanders did all they could to ensure that their men, no matter where they were able to enjoy the Christmas feast.

*****

Bob Hope and his bevy of beautiful starlets were in Vietnam entertaining the troops during the holiday season; a tradition that Bob Hope had started during World War II. The day after Christmas, Bob Hope and his troupe entertained the troops in Dong Tam. I authorized the two company commanders at Camp Viking to send as many men as they could spare without jeopardizing full security of the base; Viking was on full alert. Several truckloads of men went off to see Bob Hope's famous Christmas show. I left Major Fleri in charge of the CP and went to Dong Tam by jeep where thousands of soldiers and officers gathered in front of a makeshift stage. Bob Hope was great, and his good jokes were as corny as always. That show helped everyone relax; even if it was but for a few minutes away from the war. The starlets were beautiful, and some had talent. From a distance we could hear machine gun and artillery fire; another of many continued combat engagements with the Viet Cong and North Vietnamese Army. Bob Hope made a clever remark that he did not invite the Viet Cong to the show; the show continued.

Figure 62 Bob Hope entertains at Dong Tam

As I was returning to Camp Viking and crossing the Bailey Bridge at the entrance to the camp, I could hear mortars and AK-47s; Camp Viking was under attack. I went directly to the guard tower, climbed it, and learned that alert tower guards saw the Viet Cong as soon as they moved out of the woods on the north side of the Binh Duc airfield. Tower guards sounded the alert. We had plastered those woods with bombs and artillery just a few nights before. The men that remained at Camp Viking were in their defensive positions and were on full alert. I coordinated the defense and saw the attackers in broad daylight as they advanced across the rice paddies between Camp Viking and the Binh Duc airfield. The engineers in the fighting bunkers opened fire with machine guns and the infantry mortar crew began dropping rounds on the Viet Cong. The Viet Cong suffered very heavy casualties and were unable to reach our outer barbed wire perimeter. They retreated, taking their dead and wounded with them.

I will never think of the Bob Hope Christmas shows without remembering how close we were to disaster if our security had not been on full alert. Our defense was sound. The Viet Cong attacked again that night with mortars and rockets causing minor damage and few more casualties.

NEW YEAR AND THE FLU

The last day of 1968 was just another busy stressful day visiting my engineers on the job. There were no New Year's Eve parties, and the first day of the year was just another day, filled with challenging work while we kept one eye out for the Viet Cong.

Another enemy attacked the battalion in January: the flu. The battalion's surgeon reported many soldiers were on the sick list with the flu. Bill Garcia and Chaplain Mills were among the sick. While those sick with the flu rested, the rest of the men pressed on with the work. On 23 January, I caught a mild case of the flu bug and spent a day at Viking, most unusual. I used the time to catch up on administrative work with the staff.

BRAVO COMPANY CHANGE OF COMMAND

Captain Robinson and his men were doing an excellent job at Cao Lanh. I was concerned about finding a qualified replacement for him when his Vietnam tour ended. It was important that I replace Robinson with a strong leader; however, I had no qualified captains available within the battalion and preferred not to assign one of our leading lieutenants to command that company. I asked the 34th Group Adjutant for help in assigning a strong leader to command Bravo Company.

Just days before Captain Robinson's departure date, the 34th Group finally responded to my request and assigned a replacement, a first lieutenant who was on the promotion list to captain. During my meeting with the new officer, I was not impressed with his demeanor and record and had doubts about his leadership. However, I made a regrettable mistake and decided to place him command of Bravo Company.

Ideally, there should have been a week or so overlap between Captain Robinson's departure and the new officer's assumption of command. That was not possible. I took the new lieutenant to Cao Lanh the next day where he, Captain Robinson, and I spent several hours walking over the entire project to acquaint the new commander with his responsibility. Once we finished that orientation late in the day, I officiated at a change of command ceremony in front of all the men in the company. I took the company guidon from Captain Robinson and gave it to the new commander. Robinson had been an excellent commander, especially during the period when faced with so many challenges at Cao Lanh. He left his company in good condition.

Robinson bid farewell to his soldiers, grabbed his duffle bag, and flew back to Camp Viking with me. He left Vietnam the next day. I left Bravo Company under the leadership of a new but unknown commander.

I returned to Cao Lanh every two days to keep a close watch on the new commander, the company, and the men's work. It was not long before I suspected that he lacked the strong character and leadership demanded of that important command. I based my opinion on the performance of his men, their appearance, and several conversations I had with the company's officers and non-commissioned officers. I talked with the company commander and told him that I was not satisfied with his leadership and work progress, and I expected him to "buck-up" and change his attitude.

When I arrived back at Cao Lanh two days later, I could see that there was no improvement in the company's operations. It was clear to me and to Sergeant Major McCurley that the men's attitude had changed; their morale was low, and their discipline was poor. Their living conditions and the base area looked terrible; security was lax, the construction schedule was slipping. The company's character had changed drastically since Captain Robinson left the company.

The commander's leadership and lack of concern for his mission and his men was unsatisfactory. Since those men's lives were my responsibility, I summoned the commander and reprimanded him for the unsatisfactory conditions. His reaction was almost hostile. I met with the First Sergeant, a veteran with many years' experience, and asked him about the personal conduct of his company commander and reminded him that the safety and security of the men was more important than his loyalty to the commander. He told me that the company commander had been absenting himself from duty, to visit the bars, and prostitutes in Cao Lanh.

I decided that I must relieve the officer from command before I left Cao Lanh that day, because I could no longer trust him. I summoned him, relieved him from command, and ordered him to get his gear and be on my helicopter by the time I was ready to leave.

I summoned Lieutenant Sorenson, the executive officer, and placed him in command of the company. I told him that I would trust him to lead his men and restore the company to its former self, and that I would return with a new commander as soon as one was available. Lieutenant Sorenson had limited experience, but he was much better than his predecessor. I told the First Sergeant that I would depend on him to support the acting commander, and that he must help hold the company together.

When I returned to Camp Viking, I placed the ex-company commander on restriction, and told my Adjutant, Captain Nutt, to contact 34th Group and have him shipped out in the morning. I told Colonel Graves about my action and told him that I must have a strong leader for Bravo Company.

I logged many hours flying to Cao Lanh every other day to meet with Lieutenant Sorenson, his officers, and leading non-commissioned officers to make sure that they had all the support they needed and to encourage them. Like so many of my fine young lieutenants, Sorenson rose to the occasion and did a first-class job in the days that followed; morale improved, good discipline returned, and the construction work was back on schedule.

Figure 63 Captain Jones commanded Bravo Company

It took several weeks before 34th Group assigned Captain Richard H. Jones to the battalion. I examined Jones' records and talked with him to evaluate his potential to lead Bravo Company. I concluded that the Army had sent me an officer that was well qualified to command a company in combat. Captain Jones went with me to Cao Lanh the next morning, and I placed him in command of Bravo Company. Jones turned out to be a fine officer and he did an outstanding job leading Bravo Company.

PLAIN OF REEDS

During those many long flights to and from Cao Lanh, I watched the sun's reflection dance along the shimmering water surface of the rice paddies and the vast grasslands of the Plain of Reeds. There was very little dry land except for the few villages along the banks of the canals. My thoughts were about our many problems, the futility of the war, the battalion's great soldiers and officers, and my dear family that I hoped to see again someday.

The vastness of the Plain of Reeds is awesome, a wetland depression of about 5,000 square miles, subject to seasonal flooding from July to December. The many canals that crisscross the Plain of Reeds provided "highways" for the local Vietnamese as well as for North Vietnamese Army to move men and

Figure 64 Mekong Delta and Plain of Reeds

equipment from Cambodia into Long An Province. It was impossible to know if a sampan carried a peaceful farmer taking crops to the market, or if it carried more guns, ammunition, and explosives to attack Camp Viking. The sampans displayed the South Vietnamese flag but that was not a sign of their loyalty.

Often, during those flights, I saw 9th Division infantrymen landing in Hueys as they attacked Viet Cong troops entrenched in tunnels and defensive positions in the canal banks. Jets and helicopter gunships supported the infantrymen.

The 9th Division's Riverine Brigade on board several Navy vessels could navigate along the length of the Mekong River and that gave the division access to enemy positions they could not reach otherwise. Our battalion often cleared mines for the Riverine Brigade.

Our combat engineers also helped US Navy swift boat clear mines in the Plain of Reeds. During one such operation, our engineers cleared hundreds of mines and found thirty-two mortars which the North Vietnamese Army had hidden.

During a few of those trips to Cao Lanh, I talked with the commander of the Special Forces Detachment to learn about enemy activity in the area, because I had no better source of intelligence. He showed me ammunition and weapons that his Green Berets captured. Every round of ammunition the Special Forces captured was a round that the Viet Cong or North Vietnamese Army would not use against us. The weapons and ammunition came all the way from Russia and China. The sight of that stockpile reminded me of the futility of the Paris Peace talks. The North Vietnamese would not stop fighting until we left Vietnam.

TAN AN AIRFIELD

The battalion was ordered to build an airfield near Tan An to support 9th Division operations in the Plain of Reeds and the area south of Saigon. The project included a runway, taxiway, a heliport, and a one-thousand-meter-long earth berm to protect the airfield operations from direct fire and observation. The project also included construction of a new access road, a large maintenance area, an ammunition storage area, helicopter revetments, and refueling and rearming areas.

Bill Garcia and I examined the airfield site to prepare estimates of the work. It would be a major earth moving operation and the project called for no vertical construction. I assigned the project to Lieutenant Jones because his 595 Engineer Light Equipment Company's large earth moving equipment was best suited to execute the work.

Lieutenant Timothy Weltin, from Fremont, Ohio, moved his platoon to the construction site and started work. His men excavated and hauled more than three-hundred thousand cubic yards of rice paddy clay during the dry season to construct the 1,000-meter berm, the airstrip, the parking and refueling areas. His dozers moved the soil for the protective berm while 290M large earth movers dug fill from rice paddies, hauled it and spread it for the road and the maintenance area.

MY DAY

Every day in Vietnam brought new tasks, more problems, sorrows, and some satisfaction. A typical day started around 05:30 hours. My first stop was the mess for some coffee, my malaria pill, a salt pill, and a quick breakfast. A typical breakfast menu included canned fruit juice, lots of coffee, eggs, milk, pancakes and sometimes we enjoyed fresh doughnuts made by the Mess Sergeant. After breakfast I went to my CP to meet with the executive officer and staff to give them last minute guidance for the day. I often received urgent orders for a new mission during the night. Launching a new mission required that I make decisions on operational matters with Bill Garcia. Since Bill and I shared the same hooch, we usually had discussed and settled most of the operational business before breakfast.

By 08:00 hours, I was ready to board a chopper which flew down from the 20th Brigade base at Long Binh. On a typical day I flew to as many of the remote job sites that time would allow. I visited each company commander at his CP as often as possible. I usually ate lunch with the men in the field or at one of the company bases. Several days a week I landed at Dong Tam to meet with Guy Jester and other officers in the 9th Division staff, and to attend the late-afternoon update for General Ewell. After a late supper back at Viking, I spent the evening in the CP with the staff and the usual stack of administrative paper work. In the evening I occasionally talked with Colonel Graves on the telephone to discuss problems and to clarify guidance which had come from his staff. The evening's work at the CP ended anywhere from 22:30 to 01:00 hours. When I got to my hooch, I read my mail from home and wrote a letter to my family. Then I took a cold shower and hit the sack. The Viet Cong. also controlled my evenings and nights. Many were the nights when we were on alert. Sometimes we had no warning. That made for many short nights.

CHARLIE COMPANY CHANGE OF COMMANDERS

I lost another one of my company commanders when Captain Joe Cidras left. He had successfully managed some of the battalion's most challenging operations. I selected First Lieutenant Stephen R. Bourke to command the company, based on his excellent performance of duty as the Support Platoon commander and the Property Book Officer in the 595 Light Equipment Company. I also moved First Lieutenant Richard E. Kent from his duty as the 2nd Platoon Leader of Bravo Company to serve Bourke as his Executive Officer. Kent replaced First Lieutenant William Brown who I assigned as executive officer for Alpha Company.

MORE CASUALTIES

January 30th was another very bad day. The Viet Cong wounded four Delta Company engineers as they supported the 2/47th Infantry in Go Cong Province. A sniper hit the 3rd Platoon Leader in the abdomen and within 20 minutes a Medevac transported him to the 3rd Surgical Hospital at Dong Tam. After the surgeons performed surgery, I received a

Figure 65 L to R LTC Peixotto, Capt. Cidras, Lt. Bourke

report that he was out of danger. The medics evacuated him to Japan the following day. The 3rd Platoon leader had been with the battalion for less than two months. Another Medevac transported the three wounded engineers to the MASH in Dong Tam. I visited them later that day. I tried to visit all the battalion's wounded engineers; I believe that was an important part of my job.

BATTALION EXECUTIVE OFFICER

Figure 66 Charlie Company change of command, LTC Peixotto passes company guidon to LT. Bourke

Paul Fleri left for Hawaii on his well-deserved R&R. His absence confirmed how valuable he was to me and to the battalion. He was second in command of the battalion. His temporary absence caused me to worry about his replacement, so I urged the 34th Group Adjutant to assign another major to the battalion before Paul's tour in Vietnam ended. The Adjutant repeatedly told me that there were no majors available.

The day before Paul left Vietnam, I presented the Bronze Star Medal to him in recognition for his outstanding performance of duty. I had recommended that he receive the Legion of Merit but the 20th Brigade's conservative policies downgraded my recommendation to the Bronze Star.

With no replacement for Paul available, I continued to conduct my daily inspections of the troops and projects in the field and then I burned a lot more midnight oil with the staff. Thanks to Paul's guidance, the members of the staff performed their duties very well.

I repeatedly asked to 34th Group executive officer, Lieutenant Colonel Lawrence, for a qualified replacement for Paul, but he said there were no majors scheduled for the 34th Group. I appealed to Colonel Graves, but he did not help. He suggested that I assign the job to Bill Garcia, but I refused because Bill's work as the Operations Officer was vitally important to the success of the battalion's operations and I had no qualified officer in the battalion that had the experience needed for such a responsible job.

After Paul had been gone for a couple of weeks, I landed at the 34th Group Headquarters at Binh Thuy while on my way back to Camp Viking after long day at Cao Lanh. I talked to Colonel Graves about several operational matters and told him that I needed an executive officer. Lieutenant Colonel Lawrence told me Major John T. Giambruno, the Operations Officer, was available. The 20th Brigade had assigned a new major who Colonel Graves assigned as the Operations Officer replacing Major Giambruno who had several months to serve in Vietnam. I knew Giambruno and thought that he could do well as my executive officer. I asked Colonel Graves to assign him to the battalion and he agreed. Giambruno reported for duty on 27 January. I was grateful to have an executive officer.

LAND CLEARING IN THE DELTA

Figure 67 Converted D-7 dozer works as a Rome Plow

During the ARVN's 9th Division (that is not a mistake) dry season offensive in the area south of the Mekong River and west of Vinh Long, the division discovered a series of Viet Cong bases, hospitals, and supply caches concealed in several heavily vegetated areas and asked for help in destroying those bases.

That mission needed a Land Clearing Team; however, there were none available because the 20th Brigade's Land Clearing Teams were committed clearing jungles north of Saigon. It was only natural that my higher headquarters would pass the new mission on to my battalion. Late in January, Colonel Graves ordered me to form a new Land Clearing Team from resources within my battalion. The 34th Group or the 20th Brigade did not issue more dozers, mechanics, and engineers to reinforce the battalion for that new mission. It was hard for me to believe that they would issue such an order, considering our commitments to the many projects already assigned. It was particularly a bitter "pill" to swallow after the 79th Group had dumped so many lousy dozers on my battalion.

Figure 68 Lt. Pedigo and one of his men

I swallowed the "pill" and set out to organize a new Land Clearing Team at a time when our dozers were committed to ongoing missions. In addition, the battalion was short of maintenance personnel.

I had no choice but to work with Lieutenant Jones and his 595 Light Equipment Company to organize a new, smaller, Land Clearing Team. We analyzed his company's commitments and decided to withdraw the dozers and engineers from the Tan An airfield construction project. That, of course, had a significant impact on our production schedule, delaying completion by more than a month.

Jones selected an excellent officer, First Lieutenant Robert Pedigo, to command the unit and his senior non-commissioned officer was Staff Sergeant Bobby D. Cruey.

Figure 69 Whenever possible I carried a hot meal to our men at isolated work sites.

They in turn selected some hardy dozer operators and mechanics and reconfigured seven D-7 bulldozers for the challenging work. Jones and his men did the impossible, they created a new Land Clearing Team.

Once Lieutenant Pedigo and his engineers had prepared for the mission, they loaded their dozers on lowboy trailers and drove west on QL-4 for about forty miles to My Thuan, where all traffic crossed the

Mekong River on ferries. Once across the Mekong River they drove on to an area between Sa Dec and Vinh Long. An infantry battalion from that ARVN 9th Infantry Division worked with Lieutenant Pedigo to ensure local security and logistic support. Captain Stephen E. Draper, the US Army Engineer Advisor to the 9th ARVN Division, achieved excellent coordination between Lieutenant Pedigo and the Division.

During February, a dry month, Pedigo and his men successfully cleared more than one thousand acres of dense, hostile jungle. The trees were smaller than those cleared by the first Land Clearing Team near the Binh San rubber plantation, but the dense heavy secondary growth gave the Viet Cong excellent cover and concealment for underground bases for two Viet Cong battalions that had occupied and dominated the area.

Figure 67 ARVN Infantry in M-113 Armored Personnel carrier providing security for LT. Pedigo's land clearing operation.

Pedigo's dozer operators uncovered and destroyed more than two-hundred underground enemy bunkers. One bunker was large enough to give cover and concealment for an entire company. The jungle eaters discovered and confiscated a large cache of rice hidden by the Viet Cong. During that operation, Pedigo's engineers discovered sixteen booby traps, and many more mines, which the Rome Plows or an 9th ARVN Division demolition team detonated. The loss of that sanctuary limited the Viet Cong and North Vietnamese Army's ability to conduct offensive operations near Sa Dec, Vinh Long, and Can Tho. A few Vietnamese civilians returned to the area to reclaim their homes and farms.

Mines and booby traps caused most of Pedigo's casualties. Shrapnel from a booby trap, triggered by a dozer, wounded Lieutenant Pedigo and Staff Sergeant Cruey; however, both men were able to return to duty after medical treatment. They repaired the damaged dozer and put it back in operation. Another booby trap wounded Timothy M. Peterson during a clearing mission east of Vinh Long. Despite that, and some mechanical problems, the Team cleared one hundred and seventy acres of jungle in eight days.

South Vietnam's President, Nguyen Van Thieu, visited the Land Clearing Team while he was visiting ARVN troops in the area. He shook hands with our men and praised them for their work.

During another land clearing operation for 9th ARVN Division, Pedigo's men cleared more than 2,500 acres of jungle growth, destroyed more than 700 bunkers, 25 enemy structures and one ten-bed hospital. The area had been another sanctuary and base for a large unit.

One of the many brave men was Private First-Class Richard Leonard of Huntington, Indiana, a Medic assigned to the Land Clearing Team. The young medic treated the casualties as well as many Vietnamese children. During the day, Leonard rode in the cabs of the Rome Plows with the operators. If a plow hit a mine or a booby trap, Leonard was the first man to reach that plow to give medical treatment to the wounded operator. He risked his own life running from one plow to the other because there were many mines scattered throughout the area.

CAN GIUOC FIRE BASE

When the dry season began, the battalion received orders to return to Can Giuoc fire base to prepare it for the coming monsoon season. I revisited the base and talked with the new commander. I saw that much of the earlier work had survived the heavy rains, but the living conditions were still deplorable, the berm needed much more work, the condition of road net and firing pads was marginal, and the drainage system needed more work. Based on my visit, I decided that the mission should include raising the elevation of the firing pads and all roads leading to and within the base by at least three feet, enlarging the berm, reengineering the drainage system, and constructing nine personnel bunkers and one ammunition bunker.

The mission was assigned to Charlie Company's 1st Platoon, led by First Lieutenant Dennis J. Rog and Platoon Sergeant Norman Tyler. They had just completed construction of another fire base. Lieutenant Rog's engineers moved their equipment and construction supplies to Can Giuoc and set up their base with the artillerymen. They reengineered the drainage system using seven thirty-foot culverts and dug many drainage ditches. The platoon built nine bunkers using 16,000 board feet of lumber heavy bridge timbers and heavy lumber that our Supply Officer had ordered and delivered. The platoon excavated and moved thousands of yards of rice-paddy clay to raise the elevation of the base by three feet and rebuild the berm. As it was for all fire bases, the 5-ton truck drivers hauled massive quantities of crushed rock from Tan An and laterite from the stock pile at Ben Luc and from the borrow pit at near Bear Cat.

The Viet Cong tried to stop the rebuilding of Can Giuoc with roadblocks and mines, which the platoon cleared every morning along with a lot of handmade mines that were very difficult to detect.

Rebuilding the Can Giuoc Fire Base was a challenge for the platoon, but they completed the work on schedule to the great satisfaction to the artillerymen that would be living there during the monsoon season.

FIRE BASE SCOTT

The 2nd Battalion, 60th Infantry Regiment and an artillery unit equipped with six 155-mm howitzers and six M-102 105 mm howitzers occupied Firebase Scott, which was thirteen kilometers east of Tan An, near the village of Tan Tru. The battalion named the base in honor of Second Lieutenant James Howard Scott who died from wounds received during combat with the Viet Cong on 5 February 1967. From Firebase Scott, the infantrymen we able to move rapidly, in Hueys, to fight countless battles with the Viet Cong and North Vietnamese Army units.

The battalion was ordered to rebuild Firebase Scott in mid-February. I flew to Scott to talk with Lieutenant Colonel James Lindsay, the battalion commander, to agree on the work needed by the battalion. The base was more than twenty thousand square meters. Housing for the troops was deplorable. The fighting bunkers were inadequate, and twelve deteriorated gun pads needed major repairs. The perimeter consisted of a barbed wire fence

Figure 68 Constructing gun pad for 155-mm howitzer

and a row of sand filled, 55-gallon steel drums. There was no berm. Rice paddies surrounded the base.

I met with the company commanders and Bill Garcia to decide which company and platoon could do the work. I decided on First Lieutenant Bethke's 2nd Platoon of Captain Mouser's Alpha Company because it was close to completing an earlier mission. Within a couple of weeks, the platoon completed that mission and moved to Firebase Scott.

Under Bethke's leadership, his engineer moved thousands of cubic yards of rice paddy silt-clay to raise the elevation of the base about five feet, constructed an all-weather road that connected the base with the village of Tan Tru. They surfaced the roads with more than one hundred 5-ton truck loads of crushed rock and laterite to create an all-weather wearing surface. Once again, the battalion's 5-ton truck drivers hauled the crushed rock and laterite from the Tan An wharf and from Ben Luc. To ensure good drainage, Bethke's engineers built a drainage system using forty-six hundred feet of steel culverts.

The engineers also rebuilt the gun pads for the six 155-mm howitzers and the six 105-mm towed howitzers. The pads were strong enough to support sustained firing during the monsoon season. They used steel anchor plates to help stabilize the M102 105-mm towed howitzers.

They tore down the old makeshift bunkers and replaced them with a command bunker, three large utility bunkers, a fire direction center, seven personnel bunkers, and seven ammunition bunkers. When their schedule allowed, the infantrymen and artillerymen worked alongside the engineers, adding many hours of valuable labor. The men worked twelve hours a day and seven days a week. That was normal for the 86th. The 2nd Platoon successfully rebuilt the base during the period from February to the end of April.

Figure 69 Construction at Fire Base Scott during dry season

The Viet Cong attacked the base eight times, and the engineers fought shoulder to shoulder with the infantrymen and the artillerymen to successfully defended the base. Some members of the platoon voluntarily pulled duty at the observation posts to give early warning of the Viet Cong's approach.

Their work and relationship with the battalion was so outstanding that it served as a model for other fire bases.

Lieutenant Colonel General Fred Mahaffey replaced Lindsay during the time we worked on that base. Mahaffey was a budding four-star general and several years later became the Commanding General of the United States Readiness Command. Years after the Vietnam War, James Lindsay commanded the 82nd Airborne Division and with four stars commanded the United States Special Operations Command.

VIET CONG ATTACK CAMP PANTHER

Viet Cong or North Vietnamese Army units attacked Camp Panther on the night of 6 February 1969. The battle lasted for one and a half hours. The enemy fired many mortar rounds into the base. One mortar round made a direct hit on the battalion's Aid Station, but it did not penetrate the solid roof built by the engineers. On that same night, the Viet Cong attacked Lieutenant Joseph Paveza and Sergeant First Class Francisco Duarte's 1st Platoon, which was bivouacked along TL-21, six kilometers to the east of Camp Panther. The men fought back from behind an earth berm that surrounded their expedient base and repulsed the Viet Cong. The engineers suffered no casualties. The emphasis on security and the requirement to prepare defenses had proven invaluable.

Eight nights later, on Valentine Day, 14 February 1969, an estimated company-size force of the North Vietnamese Army or Viet Cong made another vicious surprise attack on Camp Panther; it was a dark moonless night. The enemy succeeded in penetrating the perimeter of the camp by cutting through the barbed wire protection, but Delta Company's Specialist 4 Charles L. Bell from Portsmouth, Ohio, was on guard duty, and heard the enemy cutting the barbed wire out to his front. Bell called the command bunker to request an illumination round and he moved his .50 caliber machine gun from its firing position inside the bunker to a position outside of the bunker where he had a better field of fire. As the flare went up, Bell saw the enemy and he opened fire with his machine gun and caught the enemy off guard. Guards in the other bunkers also opened fire on the Viet Cong. During the following ferocious ninety-minute battle, the Viet Cong unleashed an arsenal of RPGs, B40 Rockets, 107-mm mortar rounds, and automatic and small weapons fire. The enemy could not advance beyond the barbed wire fence and finally withdrew, badly beaten. They had counted on surprise, but due to the alertness of Specialist Bell and three other guards in his bunker, the Viet Cong lost their chance for success.

The infantrymen and engineers suffered several casualties that Medevac choppers evacuated, but miraculously there were no fatalities, thanks partially to the bunkers built by the engineers. The enemy left twenty-five of their own dead behind in their hasty retreat. They usually carried their dead with them.

It was the joint opinion of the engineers and the infantrymen that the U.S. casualties would have been staggering without the new bunkers. They had withstood the brunt of the surprise attack and afforded the precious seconds needed to launch a counter attack.

Four engineers received the Bronze Star Medal from the 9th Division for their valor. Had it not been for their alertness and initiative in moving the machine gun and calling for illumination, the enemy could have broken into the camp.

*****

One night in February, the tower guards at Camp Viking spotted about twenty or more Viet Cong assembling near the edge of the woods to our north. The Viet Cong did not realize that we could see them through our night vision equipment. I contacted the Fire Coordination Center to make sure that there were no friendly US or ARVN patrols in front of our base. When they gave us the go-ahead our machine guns and the Dusters opened fire on the unsuspecting Viet Cong. It was a very quiet night after that brief encounter, but we knew that they would be back. I do not know how many VC we killed that night, or any other time, because I did not send a patrol out to count bodies. That would have risked the lives of our men.

R&R

The Army authorized all officers and enlisted men to take a few days Rest and Relaxation (R&R) in Hawaii or in Bangkok, Thailand. Very few men passed up that opportunity to get away from the war. Libby and I had planned for our reunion for several months. Once we selected a date, Libby bought her airline tickets, and I reserved one of the private guest quarters at Fort DeRussey on Waikiki Beach.

I left the battalion on 16 February, confident that Major Giambruno and Bill Garcia would take care of the battalion during my absence. While Williams was driving me to Long Binh to catch my airplane flight to Hawaii, Giambruno called on the radio to report the death of a Delta Company Platoon Sergeant.

During that long flight to Hawaii it was difficult to stop thinking about my responsibilities and worrying about our men. After a flight of fourteen hours, the plane landed and as I came off the plane my dear wife met me; the war vanished from my mind. During those precious few days in Hawaii, I was able to compartmentalize the war and enjoy our time together. After an emotional farewell, I boarded the plane for the fourteen-hour flight back to Vietnam. I did not look forward to returning to the war.

My reliable jeep driver, Williams, met me at Long Binh. It was late in the day, but I wanted to return to Camp Viking although there was a warning that the Viet Cong was active along QL-4. I decided to head for Camp Viking at top speed and pray for a safe trip. I thank God and Williams' excellent driving for a safe trip. As we entered the base, the sun was setting. I was back in the war.

I threw my bag in my hooch and headed straight for my CP to get an update on operations. The first thing that Major Giambruno told me was that the 9th Division Intelligence section warned there would be a Viet Cong attack that night. The base was on alert and the men were prepared.

COLONEL ROLAND PEIXOTO

Next, I learned that my brother's helicopter had crashed in the jungle near An Loc. Roland was the Senior Advisor for Binh Long Province based out of An Loc. I was unable to learn about his injuries, but it was so serious that Medics had already evacuated him to a major hospital in Japan. I was anxious but helpless. It was impossible to get information about his condition from either the Army or the Red Cross. Several days passed before I learned that the crash broke his back and they evacuated him to a hospital in CONUS.

After I returned to the US, I learned that after his chopper went down in the jungle, Roland crawled some distance to reach a clearing where he hoped a rescue-chopper could see him. He kept half-hidden in the tall grass because Viet Cong were in the area. When it turned dark, he used the flame of his cigarette lighter to signal his location as a search helicopter flew over, but they did not see him as he used up all his lighter fluid. Later, the search chopper returned to the area and the chopper crew happened to see a spark from the flint of his lighter. They landed to pick him up and they found the other survivors of the crash. The chopper pilot flew the survivors directly to a MASH.

After an extended period of recuperation Roland was able to return to full duty and served as an instructor in the Command and General Staff College, and then continued a full and distinguished career in the Army.

*****

The night I returned from R&R, ten large rockets landed within the perimeter of Viking causing some damage to equipment; however, there were no casualties because the men were prepared and under cover. The men stayed in their fighting positions and waited for an attack; however, one did not materialize. The enemy continued using mortars and rockets to hit Camp Viking and the city of My Tho for three more nights. I do not know how many casualties there were in My Tho.

It seems ironic that men carried those rockets and mortar rounds all the way down the Ho Chi Minh Trail, but they did not use them effectively. It is my opinion that the enemy in the Delta was poorly trained and their marksmanship was poor. I owe my life to their poor marksmanship.

The Viet Cong, reinforced by North Vietnamese Army units continued their attacks on the My Tho and Camp Viking. Some 9th Division and the 7th ARVN Division patrols broke up several enemy formations before they could organize for an attack. However, the enemy melted into the population only to return the next night.

RACH KIEN FIREBASE

Midway through the dry season, I received orders to restore the condition of an artillery fire support base near the village of Rach Kien, which is half way between Ben Luc and Can Giuoc. The six towed howitzers at Rach Kien fired missions seven day a week to support the division's infantrymen as they fought the Viet Cong and North Vietnamese Army.

Bill Garcia went with me to Rach Kien to evaluate the conditions and prepare an estimate of the work needed to ensure that the base would be capable of sustaining operations during the next monsoon season. The conditions of the base were typical of most fire bases. The surface elevation of the roads and the entire base was too low and subject to flooding during the monsoon season. The drainage system was inadequate needing a complete new system. The artillerymen needed seventeen live-in bunkers and some ammunition bunkers. Six new M102 105-mm towed howitzer firing pads were needed

Figure 70 Towed Howitzer on firing pad

to replace the older poorly made firing pads. Large volumes of rock and laterite were needed to surface the roads and to rebuild the artillery firing pads. Also, the base needed a by-pass road for civilian traffic to keep civilians away from the base.

I assigned the task to Lieutenant Stephen R. Bourke's Charlie Company, who assigned the mission to

his 1st Platoon. I do not have a record of the platoon leader's name. Those engineers moved to the base and executed their mission on schedule and much to the satisfaction of the "customer," the artilleryman at the base. They had worked hard and met all the criteria I had set for them.

As usual, there was plenty of Viet Cong activity to attack the base which posed a great threat to their operations. The worst attack occurred on 8 March, when a rocket landed close men of 1st Platoon as they were rebuilding the access road, killing one of our engineers and wounding three others. A medevac moved the three engineers to the hospital in Long Binh.

*****

The next morning at Ben Luc, Chaplain Mills, Lieutenant Bourke, and I conducted another emotion-draining memorial service with the men from Charlie Company in memory of our fallen comrade.

After the memorial service, I talked with Lieutenant Bourke and his First Sergeant, Lucion L. Cowart, about their difficulties in supporting their 5-ton trucks, and then drove on to the 3rd Field Hospital in Long Binh to visit the three men wounded by the rocket. Two of them were in good spirits and recovering from shrapnel wounds in their arms and shoulders. The third engineer received a serious wound in the abdomen and was in surgery. I waited for the completion of the operation. The doctors told me that he would survive, but they would evacuate him to the US for more surgery and to convalesce. I was able to speak with him and through his pain and suffering the young soldier told me that he was glad that he would be going home to his family. The war was over for him. That was a tough way to get an early ticket for home.

On my way back to Camp Viking, I stopped at the Tan An bridge to check on progress. I returned to Camp Viking and inspected the 595 Light Equipment Company's facilities and equipment. Supper that night consisted of a grilled ham and cheese sandwich, stewed tomatoes, and canned peaches.

*****

I met Guy Jester and Ralph Sievers in Dong Tam on 11 March to coordinate the work of our three battalions. Ralph's battalion was still fully committed building facilities in Dong Tam. Guy's battalion was working in Dong Tam and was supporting the three brigades and many battalions throughout Long An and Dinh Tuong Provinces. My units were all over the Delta. The three of us managed to coordinate our operations and keep the Division Commander satisfied.

BINH DUC AIRFIELD

The rarely used Binh Duc airstrip was about 300 yards north of Camp Viking, across the rice paddies. The dirt runway was capable of handling Army fixed-wing airplanes and helicopters. Both the Binh Duc and Dong Tam runways were too short to accommodate larger cargo planes like an Air Force C-130. The 9th Division needed a C-130 capable airfield and the "brass" decided to construct one at the Binh Duc airstrip.

The airfield's dimensions were to be 2,300 feet long with a 200-foot overrun at both ends for a total of 2,700 feet. The width of the runway was to be 60 feet. The requirement included a turnaround area and a taxiway to connect the runway to a parking apron. The total surfaced area was greater than 300,000 square feet. When completed, the airfield would be the third largest in the Mekong Delta.

The 34th Group assigned that mission to the battalion. One of Charlie Company's platoons and men and equipment from the 595 Light Equipment Company performed most of the work.

Construction of a heavy-duty runway normally requires enormous quantities of crushed rock, sand, or laterite; however, that was not possible because massive quantities of granular materials needed for the airfield exceeded the battalion's 5-ton trucks hauling capacity, and that would have diverted those materials from other high priority missions. Construction of an airfield without granular material was an engineering challenge. The only material available in enough quantities was the silty-clay material in the rice paddies. However, that soil, by itself, could not to support the heavy load of the landing wheels of many C-130 aircraft.

The solution to that problem came from the Corps of Engineers Waterways Experiment Station in Vicksburg Mississippi. Its engineers had learned that they could mix lime with the silty-clay to make a stronger base when they moistened the silty-clay mixture to a specific moisture content. Civilian contractors had successfully used the clay-lime procedure to rebuild the western section

Figure 71 French Eiffel Bridge in Binh Phuoc

of QL-4. The battalion was the first engineer unit to apply the clay-lime process.

Prior to my arrival in August, the battalion began construction of the Binh Duc airstrip using the 595 Light Equipment Company's large earth moving equipment to excavate, transport, and distribute more than 100,000 cubic yards of silty-clay on the runway, the overrun, taxiways, and parking apron to raise the surface of the runway several feet above the expected high-water level of the Mekong River.

Once the silty-clay material was in place on the runway, the engineers placed hundreds of bags of lime about 3 feet apart over the entire surface area of the runway. Once the bags were in place, they opened them and spread the lime over the surface of the silty-clay. During the next step, a motorized grader mixed the lime with the top six to nine inches of silty-clay to achieve a four and a half percent a mixture of lime with the silty-clay material. Of course, perfection was far from possible under the circumstances. Once they completed the mixing process, 5-ton trucks with large water tanks mounted in the bed of the trucks sprayed water as evenly as possible to achieve a moisture content of from twenty-two to thirty-two percent. Quality control was difficult, particularly without a soils laboratory available; however, the young engineers did their best to meet the specifications.

Once they achieved the proper soil-water content, several heavily loaded 5-ton trucks and one smooth-wheeled roller passed over the material to compact it. The next step of the process was to seal the compacted clay-lime base from the rains by adding one layer of sand over the entire surface and then distributing asphalt on the sand. They repeated the process to ensure full coverage.

The last step was to lay more than 17,000 pieces of the M8-A1 steel landing mats on the runway, turnaround, taxiway, and parking area. Each section of landing mat weighed about 150 pounds. It was backbreaking work in the boiling sun. The hard-working engineers completed that mission early in December 1968.

DUC RIVER BRIDGE

Before the 2/47th Infantry could begin the Go Cong offensive, it was necessary for Delta Company to remove the old Class 8 French Eiffel Bridge that crossed the Duc River and then replace that bridge with a Bailey bridge. The Duc River cut through the center

Figure 72 Baily Bridge installed on the Duc River

of the village of Binh Phuoc. The Viet Cong left the old Eiffel Bridge intact because it was useful to them and the population. The old French Eiffel Bridge was too narrow and not strong enough to support our M-113s and other heavy equipment of a mechanized infantry battalion.

Engineers, armed with welding torches, went to work to cut the Eiffel Bridge in half. The next step was to drag each half of the old bridge to its respective side of the river. On the east bank, a 5-ton dump truck successfully pulled the eastern half of the bridge out of the way. On the west bank, a tank retriever pulled the bridge half to the bank, but the steel pier that supported the bridge collapsed and the bridge fell into the river. It took the power of the tank retriever and a D-7 bulldozer to drag the western half of the bridge from the riverbed. Curious villages gathered to watch the spectacle. The engineers installed a floating aluminum footbridge for the townspeople to walk from one section of the village to the other section.

Delta Company's 3rd Platoon, led by Platoon Sergeant Donald R. Cummins, constructed new abutments on both shores to shorten the gap across the river from 167 feet to 120 feet. Using a rough terrain crane, they drove a series of woodpiles fifteen feet long into the riverbank and then back-filled the area behind the pilings with rock and laterite, compacted in 6-inch lifts.

A 20th Brigade Bridge Company delivered the components of a Bailey bridge to Binh Phuoc, and less than 24 hours after they removed the old bridge, Delta Company was able to launch a Class 30 triple-single Bailey Bridge over the Duc River.

GO CONG PROVINCE

The 2/47th wasted no time as they drove their M-113s and other vehicles across the new bridge and began combat operations in Go Cong Province to clear the Viet Cong from their sanctuaries. Two platoons from Delta Company conducted combat engineer support missions for the infantry task force. On two occasions, the engineers were committed as infantry during Viet Cong attacks. During the next three months, the engineers neutralized 370 enemy bunkers, hundreds of booby-trapped roadblocks, and hundreds of mines along TL-21.

The Viet Cong did all they could to delay or halt the advancing infantrymen from entering their long-time sanctuary. They had cratered TL-21 and dug large holes that the monsoon rains had filled with water. The engineers reconstructed that road under very difficult conditions and frequent clashes with local Viet Cong agents. All the dozers available to the company excavated the silty-clay from the adjacent rice paddies to raise the surface of the road and to fill the many holes. The last step was to surface the road with truckloads of laterite. There again, our overworked drivers and fleet of 5-ton dump trucks transported thousands of cubic yards of the laterite from Ben Luc and from Bear Cat. In the meantime, those overworked 5-ton trucks were breaking down; the lack of vitally needed repair parts delayed repairing the trucks, reducing the number of trucks available for the mission.

Figure 73 Assembling a Bailey Bridge

Figure 74 Bailey Bridge ready for launching across the river on Route TL-21

The Viet Cong had destroyed two key bridges along TL-21. The first bridge crossed a river about six kilometers east of Binh Phuoc. Delta Company's engineers assembled a one-hundred-thirty-foot double-panel Bailey Bridge and launched it across the river where it rested on a newly prepared abutment. Later they replaced the Bailey bridge by constructing a wood pile-and-timber trestle bridge. The Bridge Company retrieved the bridge parts, for future use. Delta's men built a perimeter fence around the bridge site to defend it from the Viet Cong and helped prepare decent living facilities for an ARVN unit responsible for the security of the new bridge.

Ten kilometers further to the east, the Viet Cong had destroyed another old bridge across the Rach Go Cong River; another delay for the 2/47th Infantry's M-113s to continue combat operations deeper into the area. The engineers removed the remnants of the old bridge and assembled an M4T6 float (pontoon) bridge in one day. A Bridge Company from Long Binh delivered that bridge. The 2/47th moved across the new bridge to resume operations against the Viet Cong. Later, Delta Company replaced the float bridge with a wooden pile-timber-trestle bridge, and then constructed a helicopter-landing pad using local fill material and surfaced it with M8-A1 steel landing mat.

A Viet Cong unit attacked the 3rd Platoon while it was working on Route 21 on 30 January. During the fight, the Viet Cong wounded four engineers. They also wounded the platoon leader in the abdomen and, within 20 minutes, a Medevac helicopter flew him to the 3rd Surgical Hospital at Dong Tam where doctors performed surgery to save his life. A few hours later, I received the good news that he was out of danger. The medics evacuated the lieutenant to Japan the following day, and later they evacuated him to the US where he could recover and later return to civilian life. He was an outstanding young officer who had been with the battalion for less than two months. I recommended the Bronze Star Medal for his leadership. Dustoff helicopters evacuated the other three men to the hospital in Dong Tam. I went to Dong Tam later that day to visit the men as soon as the doctors stabilized their condition. I visited most of the battalion's wounded that medics evacuated to a nearby hospital; that was an important part of my job.

FEEDER ROADS

Delta Company's engineers rebuilt several feeder roads in Long an Province. One road, south of Binh Phuoc, was impassable for eight-kilometers. Earth berms or curbs along both sides of the dirt road prevented water from draining off the road. That French-design may have been good in France, but it was stupid to construct a road like that in Southeast Asia. The water-filled sections of the road looked more like a canal. Delta's engineers cut the berms, drained the water, and rebuilt the road.

The Viet Cong did all they could to stop the work by planting many mines and setting booby traps, which the engineers removed every day. Tragically, they missed one of those booby traps on an old bridge, and that cost the life of an engineer non-commissioned officer and three men wounded. A Medevac transported the wounded engineers to the MASH in Dong Tam. One of our finest non-commissioned officer lay dead. I had talked with him and his platoon at the bridge site two days prior to the incident. The next day, the platoon constructed a forty-five-foot dry-span bridge to replace that old bridge.

Delta Company's 2nd Platoon, led by Second Lieutenant Brady and Platoon Sergeant Thomas Levi, restored another of those feeder roads connecting to *Thunder Road*. His engineers constructed a timber trestle bridge to replace an old bridge that the Viet Cong had booby-trapped. That road work was more for the farmers, a part of the pacification program and not primarily for tactical purposes

*****

Delta Company engineers rebuilt several more roads and bridges that led to rich agricultural areas and villages in Long An and Go Cong Provinces. Brigadier General Gunn, the Assistant Division Commander, the Colonel Nu the Province Chief, and the District Chief cut a ribbon to officially open the roads at a ceremony attended by the local villagers.

NVA ATTACKS IN MARCH

We learned that there was as "well-organized North Vietnamese unit" active around Dong Tam and My Tho. On Saturday 8 March, patrols from the 9th Division contacted that unit as it was moving in our direction. We were prepared, so when they did attack I called for an air strike. Two jets placed several high explosive bombs in the target area and finished with several napalm bombs that covered the area with flames. Some tenacious North Vietnam Army soldiers survived and continued to fight. A C-47 circled over the area for two hours illuminating the target area with parachute flares to expose the enemy so Cobra

Figure 77 Exploding mines on TL-21

gunships could attack them. The unit finally withdrew, but they returned the next night to attack with mortars and rockets to show they had not been defeated. Several of the larger rockets struck inside the camp, resulting in casualties who we evacuated to the hospital in Dong Tam.

ALPHA COMPANY CHANGE OF COMMAND

Captain Thomas Mouser commanded Alpha Company as his engineers constructed Camp Viking, many other projects. At his departure at the end of his twelve months of service in Vietnam, I officiated at the change of command and placed First Lieutenant Dennis J. Rog in command of Alpha Company. Rog's superior performance as a platoon leader earned him the new command.

DINH TUONG PROVINCE

As the work at Cao Lanh was nearing completion under the leadership of Captain Richard H. Jones and his Executive Officer, First Lieutenant Albert Sorenson, Colonel Graves ordered the battalion to start new work near Vinh Long and in Dinh Tuong Province. I directed Captain Jones to move Bravo Company's CP and two platoons to set up a base near Vinh Long and begin work. One platoon remained at the Cao Lanh airfield until mid-June to complete the construction of several more helicopter landing pads to enable rearming of Cobra gunships, build a berm to surround the pads on three sides, upgrade the overruns, spread Peneprime on the shoulders of the runway and around the chopper pads to minimize the dust, and prepare a berm for the storage of ammunition and POL. The work did not go well because the Platoon Leader lacked experience to manage the complex project. I sent Bill Garcia to get the job back on track.

CHIEF OF ENGINEERS VISIT

Lieutenant General Cassidy, the Chief of Engineers, inspected engineer troops and engineer activities in Vietnam in March of 1969. He arrived at Camp Viking on 20 March, accompanied by Colonel Parfitt and Colonel Graves. The battalion staff presented a well-rehearsed twenty-minute briefing about the battalion's operations. We then flew to inspect one of Delta Company's platoons supporting the 2/47th Infantry in Go Cong Province. I selected that unit because of the diversity of their work and its part in the pacification program. Captain Andy Dykes gave the Chief an excellent briefing about his company's mission, its experiences, and its security. General Cassidy's visit lasted about two and a half hours. Everything went well. Colonel Graves and Colonel Parfitt seemed to be pleased.

Figure 78 Capt. Dykes describes Delta Company operations to General Cassidy.
L to R Capt. Dukes, LTC Peixotto, Col. Parfitt, General Cassidy

A SCHOOLHOUSE

As if the engineers did not have enough to do, they took part in the pacification program by building a two-room brick schoolhouse near Binh Phuoc at the request of Colonel Nu, the Province Chief. Pacification projects helped show the Vietnamese in the village that the Americans were their friends and were there to help them. The 3rd Platoon under the leadership of Platoon Sergeant Robert Cummings executed the civic action project.

MEDCAP

Our battalion surgeon, Captain Robert Falkner, and his number one medic, Specialist 4 Clarence Volk, gave medical treatment to Vietnamese civilians in the small villages during a MEDCAP operation. Captain Falkner and his medics treated three to four hundred Vietnamese every month on MEDCAP operations. Infantrymen from 2/47th escorted the doctor and his medic to ensure their security while they treated the civilians. It was normal to go unannounced to prevent a Viet Cong welcoming committee. Once they arrived at a village, the Vietnamese passed the news to everyone within a matter of minutes. The entire population of the villages received some type of treatment; the Viet Cong had left them with no medical support. The escorting infantrymen treated the children to a Mickey Mouse cartoon using a projector set up in a nearby store.

*****

Captain Andrew A. Dykes commanded Delta Company throughout the entire operation, except for two weeks in February 1969 when he left on emergency duty. His cousin had been killed in action and Andy escorted the body back to his family in the US. First Lieutenant Larry W. Warden assumed command in Andy's absence. From their arrival at Binh Phuoc, from early December to February, Delta Company sustained 17 casualties including two officers.

FIRE BASE SCHROEDER

By the end of March, the temperature and the humidity began to rise, signaling a gradual change from the dry season to monsoon season. The first rains fell on 3 April. The light rain helped settle the dust, but it was a precursor of things to come.

The 2nd Battalion of the 39th Infantry Regiment Battalion occupied Fire Base Schroeder, in western Dinh Tuong Province along Highway

QL-4. The base was on the eastern edge of the Plain of Reeds, known to be teeming with Viet Cong units. The battalion named the base in honor of Lieutenant Colonel Donald B. Schroeder, the battalion's fallen commander who was killed in action on 13 February 1969. During their 31 months in Vietnam the 2/39th Infantry Battalion suffered 256 fatalities and distinguished themselves with two Medal of Honor recipients.

Figure 79 Fire Base Schroeder

Colonel Graves ordered me to complete construction of Schroeder. Guy Jester's 15th Engineers had started the work before, so the infantry could occupy it as rapidly as possible. I inspected the condition of the base and talked with the battalion commander and members of his staff to decide on what it was that our engineers could and could not do to improve of the base.

I assigned the mission to Lieutenant Rog's Alpha Company, and he assigned the mission to First Lieutenant Clay's 3rd Platoon. Clay and Platoon Sergeant Coeburn's first task was the creation of an eight-foot high earth berm around the perimeter of the base to protect the men, artillery, and ammunition from direct fire. The hard-working operators of the platoon's bulldozers, front loaders, and 5-ton trucks worked steadily under conditions exposed to the Viet Cong to move silty-clay soil from near-by dry rice paddies. In addition, drivers of the 5-ton trucks hauled more than forty thousand cubic yards of fill into *Schroeder* to raise the elevation of the interior of the base and the access road. The engineers constructed six firing positions for the artillery battery of six 105 mm towed howitzers. The men rushed to complete the earthwork before the end of the dry season, because it would be virtually impossible to move that rice paddy soil after it turned to mud. The 3rd Platoon also installed five rows of perimeter security wire around the base.

To speed construction of twenty heavy wooden bunkers and minimize work at the distant fire base, Guy Jester and I decided his battalion would construct the bunkers in Dong Tam and airlift them to

Schroeder using CH47 Chinook helicopters. The helicopters lowered the bunkers onto the prepared positions, disconnected, and flew back to Dong Tam for another bunker. The twelve by twelve-foot bunkers would sleep twelve men and provide security for the troops during mortar and rocket attacks. They were not spacious, but they protected the weary infantrymen while they rested. Lieutenant Clay's engineers constructed a twenty-five by twenty-five-foot bunker for the Tactical Operations Center, because it was too heavy for the CH-47 helicopter.

Lieutenant Clay's 3rd Platoon supported the 2/39th Infantry during thirty-seven combat support missions to detect and destroy mines and booby traps. On one of those missions they discovered a VC stash: Chinese machine guns, three 120-mm mortars, and over five thousand rounds of small arms ammunition.

HEROIC RESCUE

Late one day, the Viet Cong ambushed and wounded two Alpha Company engineers on QL-4 while they were driving a 5-ton truck back to Camp Viking from Fire Base Schroeder. The story of their rescue is dramatic and testifies to the courage of a team of Rangers from Echo Company of the 75th Infantry who volunteered to make that nighttime rescue. Staff Sergeant Joseph F. Broudreau of Rockland, Massachusetts and his five Rangers flew out of Dong Tam at night in a blackened slick to the area where our men had reported the ambush, about 12 miles northwest of Dong Tam along QL-4. The slick circled the area where the ambush occurred and received heavy fire from the Viet Cong. The Rangers probed the area with a searchlight from the helicopter and spotted the 5-ton dump truck. They continued to search, risking more ground fire from the Viet Cong, and finally saw the two wounded engineers. As the Rangers landed their helicopter, two of the Rangers ran to save the two wounded engineers and carry the back to the helicopter, while the other Rangers provided covering fire with their machine guns and automatic weapons to keep the Viet Cong at a distance. The slick took off and flew to the MASH chopper pad in Dong Tam where doctors treated the engineers' wounds. It was a brave and dangerous mission successfully completed.

FIRE BASE DANGER

Fire Base Danger was the base for the 4th Battalion of the 39th Infantry Regiment (4/39th Infantry), the *Recondos*. The base was in western Dinh Tuong Province between Rach Ba Lam and Rach Chanh in a wide expanse of rice paddies. The division selected the site for the *Recondos* to interdict the North Vietnamese Army's infiltration routes and find their sanctuaries in the Plain of Reeds.

Lieutenant Colonel David H. Hackworth, commander the 4/39th Infantry Battalion, authored a well-read book, *About Face,* which gives an excellent account of his battalion's experiences in Vietnam. It is one of the few good accounts about the heroic infantrymen who fought the war in the Mekong Delta. I strongly recommend reading that book to get a much better view of the Vietnam than I could tell.

During my first trip to Danger, I saw the base was in very poor condition with minimal perimeter security, inadequate firing pads for the artillery, little to no overhead protection for the infantry and artillerymen, and more. There was a lot of work for a platoon.

I assigned the mission to Captain Jones's Bravo Company and his 3rd Platoon, led by First Lieutenant Branin, carried out the mission. Branin and his men found that the fire base was nothing more than a dried-up rice paddy that would become inundated as soon as the monsoon season began. According to Hackworth, a unit of the 15th Combat Engineers and one of Hackworth's rifle companies had pushed up the earth to produce a "four-sided sodden fort."

Figure 80 Fire Base Danger

Lieutenant Branin's platoon's first task was to raise the interior ground elevation well above the monsoon water level using the platoon's bulldozers, front loaders, and 5-ton dump trucks to excavate soil from the rice paddies. They also increased the elevation of the berm to ten-feet and constructed six firing positions, for the six 105 mm towed howitzers, using a standard design to ensure a stable base for the howitzers and enable them to fire in any direction. Overall, the 3rd Platoon moved more than twenty-five thousand cubic yards of dry rice paddy soil. To ensure drainage of the interior of the base, they built more than six hundred feet of culvert. The engineers added watchtowers on the berm and mounted radars to detect Viet Cong movement.

Lieutenant Branin's engineers constructed thirty ten-by-thirty-foot personnel bunkers to protect the men during mortar attacks. The platoon emplaced a heavy concertina-wire barrier that surrounded the base and, as was the custom, they filled that area with booby traps, trip flares, and claymore mines. The also developed the helicopter pads outside the base perimeter.

The engineers supported the 4/39th Infantry Battalion during many operations against Viet Cong and North Vietnamese units. During that operation, the *Recondos* killed two thousand five hundred Viet Cong.

ARVN BATTALION

As the North Vietnam Army and Viet Cong strengthened their forces in our area, the 7th ARVN Division moved an infantry battalion into the old base on the western flank of Camp Viking. I welcomed the battalion commander, Major Tap, and helped his battalion with supplies and construction material to set up their base camp. The soldiers' families lived and traveled with them. I believe that was better than leaving their families in their villages at the mercy of the Viet Cong. The ARVN battalion had very limited resources to make the men and their families comfortable.

During my first assignment in Vietnam, I ate many meals with my Vietnamese counterparts. Their food was good, and I enjoyed their hospitality. I did all I could do to cement relations between our two Armies. The Vietnamese are a kind and friendly people. The problem was their appalling lack of sanitation. I saw soldiers wash our dishes in a ditch filled with dirty, polluted water. The multiple exposures to germs caused me to contract a serious case of hepatitis. I was deathly sick and confined to bed for about six weeks before I was able to fly to Saigon to see the medics. Once they diagnosed my condition, the doctors evacuated me to a hospital in the United States where I gradually regained my health and was able to return to duty.

On my second Vietnam tour I tried to avoid eating with my Vietnamese counterparts. Thus, when Major Tap invited me to have dinner with him at a restaurant in My Tho my reaction was to decline. However, I knew that I could not refuse the invitation, because I would insult him, and I wanted to ensure a close working relationship with my new neighbor. It was to our benefit to have his infantry battalion working in our vicinity. I accepted Major Tap's invitation and enjoyed a delicious meal and a pleasant evening. I invited him to have supper at our mess and to meet my officers. His battalion had fought in many regions of the Delta. As it turned out, his battalion spent most of their time in the field, so they added very little to the security of Camp Viking.

FIRST LIEUTENANT PEIXOTTO

Figure 81 My Tho

My nephew, First Lieutenant David E. Peixotto, arrived in the country and was assigned to the 168th Engineer Battalion, one of five battalions assigned to the 79th Engineer Group. David graduated from West Point in 1967 and, like his father, had chosen a career in the Corps of Engineers. David was born in 1944 while his father, then an Engineer Lieutenant, was part of General Patton's Third Army fighting its way across France. The news of David's assignment reminded me that the officers serving in my battalion were about his age. What they lacked in experience, most of them made up in courage and plain smarts. Soon after his arrival, David was able to catch a flight to Camp Viking for a brief visit.

A WORM'S EYE VIEW OF THE WAR

From my worm's eye view of the war, I was troubled that there were no obvious signs that we were winning the war in Vietnam. The bombing halt in the north did not change conditions in Delta. The lack of a clear victory, coupled with the lack of popular support for the war, troubled me. I tried not to concern myself with the big picture because there was nothing I could do about the situation. I focused on carrying out the battalion's missions and protecting the lives of my men.

What I did not realize at that time was that our politicians had already given up any hope of winning the war. Secret negotiations were underway with North Vietnam. The North Vietnamese won the negotiations because the United States had already decided that we were going to withdraw and turn the war over to the South Vietnamese. Those of us in Vietnam kept fighting and more men died; unknown to me, we had lost the war.

PERSONNEL ISSUES

It was not possible for me to know exactly how many of my engineers used drugs. We disciplined men caught smoking drugs. The best indicator of drug usage was the record of punishments under the UCMJ. For example, during a three-month period, the battalion had sixty-one cases of punishment under article 15, UCMJ. Six of those cases involved drugs. The men did not believe that they had been doing anything wrong; that is common in our society. I told our non-commissioned officers and officers that we must not tolerate the use of drugs.

*****

One month the medical report revealed a minor increase in the battalion's venereal disease rate. Our rate was always lower than the other battalions in the Group, and most units in Vietnam, but the 34th Group staff pounced on the increase and required

Figure 82 ARVN Soldiers on TL 21

that I report what actions I was taking

to correct the situation. To be truthful, I had very little influence on the situation. I believe one reason the battalion had a low rate was that the men worked hard and had little access to women where they worked. The battalion's medics helped control the venereal disease rates with a program of instruction for personnel, combined with the pursuit and treatment of the sources of the disease.

REBUILD ROUTE 227

The Long An road improvement program was a continuous series of projects to open one secondary road after the other. The 2nd Platoon of Charlie Company rebuilt nine and one-half kilometers of Route 227 that passed through a Viet Cong sanctuary. The road had been impassible since 1963. On my preliminary reconnaissance I saw a narrow path which used to be a two-lane road. The Viet Cong had cut the road with about ninety craters and trenches; the rains did the rest.

Before the work could begin, the 2nd Platoon cleared more than one-hundred mines and booby traps. After they removed the mines and booby traps,

Figure 83 A Combat Engineer

the engineers checked for new mines every morning before work began, because the Viet Cong returned every night and buried more mines and booby traps. They replaced an old damaged bridge with a forty-five-foot dry-span bridge that the 15th Engineers assembled by in Dong Tam and delivered to the bridge-site by a CH-54 Flying crane helicopter. The big chopper carefully lowered the big bridge onto the previously prepared abutments. The platoon installed many culverts along the route to control the flow of water from one side of the road to the other. After moving thousands of cubic yards of native fill to rebuild the base of the road, our 5-ton truck drivers delivered crushed rock and laterite to create a wearing surface.

During another similar project, Charlie Company upgraded five kilometers of road near Ben Luc using more rock and laterite, and they built a Class 35 timber trestle bridge across a small river.

BRIDGING THE RACH CHANH RIVER

First Lieutenant Roger D. Smith, Charlie Company's 3rd Platoon Leader and Platoon Sergeant Joseph Broadstone led their platoon as they replaced a demolished bridge over the Rach Chanh River with a Class 40 timber trestle bridge, 160 feet long. The bill of materials for the bridge called for 46,000 board feet of lumber, 81 wood piles 50 feet long, 400 linear feet of cyclone fencing, plus laterite and rock for the approaches and back fill for the abutments.

The men used a rough terrain crane to drive 81 piles. The shortage of rough terrain cranes delayed the start of work by nineteen days. There were several cranes in the battalion but most of them were deadlined, awaiting parts. That was another example of the supply system delaying our work.

The Viet Cong attacked the platoon several times while working on the bridge. The engineers dropped their tools and picked up their weapons to engage the enemy from defensive positions. The men worked on that bridge and the road from mid-March to early May.

MACV ADVISOR HOUSING

Most of the US Army MACV advisors were stationed in small villages to advise their ARVN units. The Senior Advisor in Long An Province appealed to me for help in improving the living conditions of his advisors. Their living conditions were far worse than ours. The 2nd Platoon of Charlie Company was assigned to the mission. The advisors in Go Den lived in a mud hut. The combat engineers were proud to help their fellow soldiers. They became carpenters, plumbers, and electricians to construct new housing at five separate locations, Rach Kien, Can Giuoc, Go Den, Tan Tru and Binh Phuoc. The finished work included billets, latrines, showers, and lighting.

NEW SUPPLY OFFICER

By the time Captain Ed Ajer departed for home, he had turned our supply operation around. He not only passed the Inspector General inspection, but he and his men continued to improve the logistics support for the battalion. I replaced Ajer with a newly assigned officer, Captain F.T. Voorstadt.

A "CAN DO" BATTALION

I was very proud of men in the battalion. As their commander, I was able to see all of them as they struggled to carry out difficult missions under stressful circumstances. They did outstanding work and were courageous. There were no Medal of Honor recipients in the battalion, but they showed great courage every day.

The battalion's official motto was *Pontificus Sumus*. The motto came from the battalion's WWII heritage when it was a float-bridge unit, supporting General Patton's Third Army as it advanced across many rivers on its way to defeating the German Army.

I believed that Latin mottos were fine, but the young soldiers knew little of the Latin language. Right or wrong, I informally changed our motto to "CAN DO." The men painted that motto on our vehicles and equipment, and on the battalion's CP sign. Colonel Parfitt was not pleased, and he challenged my action because I had not asked permission to change the battalion's motto. Although the motto was not original, it boosted pride and morale.

*****

Two battalion commanders left the 34th Group in March. Lieutenant Colonel Ralph Sievers passed his battalion colors to Lieutenant Colonel Jack Plunkett at a ceremony in Dong Tam with Major General Ewell and Major General Parker present. Lieutenant Colonel Rich Leonard left the 35th Construction Battalion but I do not have any notes about his replacement. The 35th was based at Vinh Long where the ceremony took place.

*****

By the end of March, the temperature and the humidity began to rise, signaling a gradual change from the dry season to monsoon season. The first rains fell on 3 April. The light rain helped to settle the dust, but it was a precursor of things to come.

ROUTE 208

Late in March, orders came to rebuild Route 208, an unpaved two lane fifteen-kilometer road which connected My Tho to Binh Phuoc. The Viet Cong had closed that road before the 1968 TET Offensive and the 7th ARVN division was clearing the Viet Cong from the area to reduce the threat to My Tho and to reopen the area. Opening Route 208 was beneficial to the pacification program because it serviced a large farming area.

Lieutenant William C. Langford's 1st Platoon of Alpha Company moved to the My Tho end of the road on 1 April and began the usual earthwork using rice paddy clay, crushed rock, and laterite.

The Viet Cong had destroyed two Eiffel bridges. When Langford's platoon began to remove the first bridge the returning villagers were so enthusiastic about the work that they pitched in and helped our men remove the old bridge and the wire entanglement around the bridge. A temporary aluminum float foot bridge provided the villagers access across the river while the platoon constructed a one-hundred and forty-four-foot timber pile bent bridge with eight spans. They added a chain link fence around the bridge piers to protect them from floating mines and enemy sappers. The Province Chief assigned a local RFPF unit to protect the completed structure.

Further north, the platoon removed another demolished Eiffel Bridge and replaced it with a one-hundred and forty-four-foot timber trestle bridge.

*****

Ten combat engineers from Alpha Company supported a US Navy swift boat unit as it cleared a minefield at Tuyen Nhomin in the Plain of Reeds. Our engineers cleared hundreds of mines and found thirty-two mortars which a North Vietnamese Army had hidden. The mortars were made in China. Engineers from Bravo Company performed a similar mission for the Riverine Brigade.

LAND CLEARING EAST OF MY THO

While Pedigo's Land Clearing Team was fully committed in the west, orders came from the 34th Group to execute another land clearing operation east of My Tho in support of the 7th ARVN Division. It was another of those unbelievable urgent mission.

Because the 595 Light Equipment Company had no more resources to squeeze out of its operations, I had no choice but to turn to Lieutenant Rog's Alpha Company to organize a second Land Clearing Team, sacrificing progress on the company's other projects with the loss of their dozers, operators, and mechanics. Lieutenant Rog succeeded in organizing a small Land Clearing Team with three dozers and it began work in April. The men cleared more than one-thousand acres of Viet Cong territory that posed a threat to My Tho and elsewhere. Next that Land Clearing Team moved on to clear five hundred acres of jungle, destroyed a small underground hospital, and forty-seven bunkers in an area to the east of My Tho.

Just as the monsoon rains were starting, the 34th Group directed me to clear the troublesome wooded area north of Camp Viking, used by the North Vietnamese Army and Viet Cong to attack our base, as well as My Tho. I was eager to start that mission. However, it was too late; the monsoon rains combined with the poor soil conditions made the task impossible and I told Colonel Graves that I cancelled the mission.

NEW DIVISION COMMANDER

The end of an era arrived on 2 April when Major General Julian Ewell relinquished command of the Division to Major General Harris Hollis. Promoted to Lieutenant General, Ewell remained in Vietnam to command the II Field Force. After a formal change-of-command ceremony in Dong Tam, I spoke with General Hollis and requested an opportunity to show him how the 86th Combat Engineer Battalion supported his division. The 86th was not an organic part of his Division, and he was not my commander; however, he was my primary customer. The division staff had not scheduled General Hollis to visit the battalion. He accepted my invitation and we met in my battalion CP to discuss the battalion's operations. General Parker, and Colonel Parfitt also attended. After eating lunch in our Headquarters Company mess tent, we flew to visit our engineers at the Tan An bridge, Fire Base Danger, and Delta Company as it supported the 2/47th Infantry in Go Cong Province. During General Ewell's time, he had not visited the 86th.

The idea for an engineer briefing mushroomed. By the time it occurred, on 23 April, General Parker, Colonel Parfitt, and Colonel Graves attended the session at the 9th Division headquarters. The engineer battalion commanders briefed: Jack Plunkett, Guy Jester, and Peixotto. The meeting was quite successful, and General Hollis was duly impressed with the amount of engineer support dedicated to support his Division.

*****

The Deputy Commander of the 20th Brigade, Colonel Wilson, visited the 86th on 10 April. That was his only visit with the battalion. Following a command briefing by the staff and lunch in the headquarters company mess, I took him to see the land clearing operation, Fire Base Danger, and the Tan An airfield.

TWO COMPANY COMMANDERS DEPART

Figure 84 General Hollis visits 86 Engineer CP. L to R LTC Peixotto, LTC Jester, General Hollis, Col. Graves

1st Lieutenant Stephen R. Bourke, the very capable commander of Charlie Company, returned to the US in late April. I selected First Lieutenant Richard E. Kent, the company's Executive Officer, to assume command of the company. I officiated at a change-of-command ceremony at Ben Luc. Kent was the third officer to command the company in nine months.

152

I also officiated at the change of command ceremony for the 595 Light Equipment Company when 1ˢᵗ Lieutenant Albert A. Sorenson assumed command from 1ˢᵗ Lieutenant Yancey L. Jones. Lieutenant Jones had performed very well and had been a strong commander. Lieutenant Sorenson had served as the Executive Officer for Bravo Company.

PEACE NEGOTIATIONS

The North Vietnamese Communists presented a ten-point peace program to our representative in Paris on 8 May 1969. In my opinion, it was not a peace plan. It was an ultimatum to the United States for an unconditional and unilateral US withdrawal from South Vietnam. They also wanted reparations for war damages. The Pacific Stars and Stripes, our primary source of daily news, hailed the proposal. From my point of view, we in Vietnam were fighting an enemy encouraged by our politicians, Hollywood celebrities, the media, and rioting young people on campuses.

Figure 85 LT. Jones

President Nixon's eight-point program to advance the American negotiating position proposed a unilateral withdrawal of American troops, but he said that the US would support the South Vietnamese Army, so they could carry on the war without the US military forces. Nixon's plan was a total capitulation that spelled the end of the war for the United States without winning. The plan called for strengthening South Vietnam's military to continue the war but, many of us in Vietnam knew that the South Vietnamese could not defeat the insurgents with their forces when the joint forces of the United States and South Vietnam could not do the job.

It seemed obvious to me that President Nixon, other politicians, and the Joint Chiefs of Staff had decided that South Vietnam was no longer worth the price.

I believe the political and military leaders in Washington never did develop a winning strategy for the Vietnam War from the time that President Kennedy transformed the United States' use of advisors and began to inject Green Beret units and helicopters in the fight. From then on, the United States gradually escalated its involvement by committing more and more combat troops, with no strategy or plan to win the war. Washington strategists worried about the "domino effect" of losing all southeast Asia but they had a greater fear of Russian and Chinese involvement. It is a shame that Presidents Kennedy and Johnson escalated the war at the cost of tens of thousands of soldiers that they drafted to defend the United States of America.

In his book, "White House Years," Henry Kissinger said that he issued a directive on 10 April for the Defense Department to work out a schedule for Vietnamizing the war.

For better or worse, the beginning of our defeat had started. I say defeat because we did not win! If you do not win, you lose!

While the politicians and the diplomats were meeting in comfort, the Viet Cong and North Vietnamese Army increased the intensity of their aggressive operations in the Delta making it obvious that Hanoi was proving that they were strong, and that they would outlast the US. I received an intelligence report that five new North Vietnamese Army units were very active in our area. The North Vietnamese Army and Viet Cong did their best to stop the joint infantry engineer operations as we extended the road nets into their sanctuaries. A North Vietnamese Army unit attacked one of our platoons and destroyed a large scoop loader with a rocket. The next day they set off a command-detonated mine under one of our loaded 5-ton dump trucks and destroyed it. The loss of equipment was not as distressing the casualties.

*****

Colonel Graves held another battalion commanders conference in Binh Thuy on Saturday 1 May.

*****

It was still dry enough in early May to continue work on all projects. The rains held off except for some minor storms. Every day of dry weather was a good day for engineer construction. We made an all-out effort to finish up our dry season missions.

A REINFORCED BATTALION

The battalion was stretched to the limit in May; however, Colonel Graves called one evening and ordered me to undertake some additional construction projects near Rach Kien in Long An Province. I flew to the project area to inspect the proposed projects, there were many and would be challenging. I decided that I would need to commit a full combat engineer company to perform the work; however, I could not begin the new projects until the battalion completed other ongoing projects. I called Colonel Graves to tell him that I would need to halt work on other priority projects to assume responsibility for the new projects.

The new projects carried such a high priority that Colonel Parfitt decided to reinforce the 86th with another combat engineer company; Delta Company of the 168th Combat Engineer Battalion.

Within two days, the company commander, Captain Antonio Janarro, arrived at Camp Viking. He, Bill Garcia, and I prepared plans for the project, and plans to support his company when it moved from their base north of Saigon to the Delta. Janarro's 1st and 2nd Platoons arrived at Rach Kien on 5 May and the 3rd Platoon arrived on 8 May. Their earlier mission had been to emplace a minefield around Long Binh and construct gun pads for the 1st Infantry Division at Lai Khe. The men had plenty of combat experience and performed their mission very well.

With the addition of Janarro's company, the battalion included seven companies with more than 1,200 men. Adding that company to my responsibilities stretched me a bit thinner.

NATIONAL GUARD COMPANY

Although I had authorized our headquarters company mechanics to perform higher echelon repairs, they were overwhelmed with deadlined vehicles and engineer equipment.

My request for maintenance support had not fallen on deaf ears. I was surprised when Colonel Graves told me that the Army had activated the 238th National Guard Maintenance Company at Fort Hood, Texas on 13 May 1968 and Colonel Parfitt assigned the company to support my battalion and other units. The 238ᵗʰ was one of a few National Guard units called to active duty during the Vietnam War.

To make room for the 238ᵗʰ, I pulled some of the 595 Light Equipment Company's equipment from the construction of the Tan An airfield to excavate thousands of cubic yards of rice paddy clay to enlarge Camp Viking.

When First Lieutenant Richard D. Hutchinson, from Fort Worth, Texas, and his advance party arrived at Camp Viking, I assigned our engineers to work with him to prepare the basic living and working facilities for his company. The men of the 238ᵗʰ had high morale and were eager to do their mission in Vietnam. Chief Warrant Officer Albert Utz of San Antonio, Texas was the Chief of the Maintenance Section of the 238ᵗʰ. Their arrival gave a great boost to our moral and slowly helped improve the availability of equipment for our missions.

DISPOSITION OF THE BATTALION

My records are not adequate to keep track of each platoon's location throughout the year. However, it is interesting to note the battalion's deployment during May. The Battalion Headquarters and Headquarters Company were at Camp Viking.

Lieutenant Rog's Alpha Company's headquarters was at Camp Viking. Lieutenant William C. Langford's 1ˢᵗ Platoon was constructing a timber trestle bridge site on Route 208 in the Ben Tranh District and First Lieutenant Bethke's 2ⁿᵈ Platoon was working to improve conditions at Tan Tru Fire Base. First Lieutenant Clay and Platoon Sergeant Coeburn's 3ʳᵈ Platoon was busy at Fire Base *Schroeder*. Land Clearing Detachment 2 was clearing an area east of My Tho.

Captain Jones' Bravo Company headquarters and the 1ˢᵗ Platoon were based at Vinh Long. The 2ⁿᵈ Platoon stayed at the base at Cao Lanh to complete that project, and First Lieutenant Branin's 3ʳᵈ Platoon was constructing Fire Base Danger.

Lieutenant Richard E. Kent's Charlie Company headquarters remained at Ben Luc and the 1ˢᵗ Platoon was working at the Fire Base at Rach Kien. Lieutenant Speed's 3ʳᵈ Platoon continued to improve the protective structures around the Tan An bridge, and the 2ⁿᵈ Platoon was working on projects from the base at Ben Luc.

Captain Dyke's Delta Company headquarters and the three Platoons were based at Binh Phuoc and continued their work on the road system, the bridges, school buildings, and combat missions.

Captain Janarro's Delta Company of the 168th Combat Engineer Battalion were starting to execute their construction mission at Rach Kien.

1st Lieutenant Albert A. Sorenson's 595 Light Equipment Company headquarters was at Camp Viking along with the 1st and 3rd Platoons. Lieutenant Timothy Weltin's 2nd Platoon was constructing the Tan An Airfield. First Lieutenant Robert Pedigo and Staff Sergeant Bobby D. Cruey led the Land Clearing Team Detachment as it continued clearing operations south of Vinh Long.

CHAPLAIN MILLS DEPARTS

Chaplain Mills received a notice from the Red Cross that his brother died in an automobile accident back in the US. Captain Nutt worked a miracle with the personnel system, and by 17:00 hours that afternoon the good Chaplain was in Long Binh, scheduled to fly out for the US that night. His early departure left us without a Chaplain.

Figure 86 Chaplain Mills hold services next to a Rough Terrain Crane

The 34th Group Adjutant told me there were no new chaplains in the personnel "pipeline." My men needed a chaplain.

I had developed a strong spiritual bond with Harold Mills. Our men lived in the face of death every day and many of them found renewed spiritual strength, as I did, in Harold Mills simple Christian services. We acknowledged that any one of us could be the next to be killed in action.

Mills' brother had been very worried about Harold in Vietnam, but he was the one who died. That is a grim reminder that more people died on the highway than died during the entire Vietnam War.

LIEUTENANT COLONEL JOE SMITH

Figure 87 LTC Peixotto and LTC Smith

My brother-in-law, Lieutenant Colonel Joseph S.C. Smith, had arrived in Vietnam late in March. Joe was my roommate at West Point for four years. The day after our graduation, I married Libby, his sister. Joe was the Engineer Advisor for the ARVN engineers in the Mekong Delta. Their headquarters was in Can Tho. My battalion performed several projects for the ARVN. There were few opportunities for us to meet. On 10 May, Joe and I visited the projects the battalion was performing for ARVN: the two land clearing operations, Route 208, and the road work in Long an Province. We also reconnoitered two new areas where ARVN had requested more engineer support.

COMMAND MAINTENANCE MANAGEMENT INSPECTION TEAM

A Command Maintenance Management Inspection Team from the 20th Brigade inspected two companies in May; both companies passed the inspection. That was an important milestone; the first time any company in the battalion had passed a Command Maintenance Management Inspection. The availability of our equipment was much better than it had been back last September.

Based on peacetime standards the battalion would still be rated, *not ready for combat.* The availability of our equipment never did achieve the Army's or my high standard. A battalion can meet those standards in peacetime with an adequate supply of repair parts, with more trained personnel, and with proper support from higher levels. However, it is not realistic to expect a unit heavily engaged to keep those standards.

*****

The guards on Camp Viking's perimeter were always on alert, twenty-four hours a day, to give us an early warning of attack. Occasionally they became a bit nervous in the lonely bunkers. One dark night an unfortunate incident occurred, when one of our engineers was moving around in an area where he should not have been. An alert guard shot him. The wound was not critical. The guard did his job and the victim was at fault.

GENERAL HOLLIS COMMENDS THE 86TH ENGINEERS

Late in May, General Hollis invited me to attend a dinner at his mess. After dinner, General Hollis spoke to his officers and was very generous in his comments about the 86th. He was a different kind of leader from General Ewell. Both men were effective division commanders, but General Hollis had much more interest in his subordinates than General Ewell.

After the dinner, I went to the helipad to board a "slick" that would take me back to Camp Viking. At that moment, several heavy rockets and mortar rounds hit the helipad. They were very close. The pilot,

Figure 88 General Hollis honors
86th Combat Engineers

crew, and I dove into a nearby bunker. Several choppers were damaged. After things calmed down, the blacked-out slick flew me to Camp Viking. A slick was a stripped-down Huey with no seats and doors. It was too dark that night for the chopper to land on the pad inside the camp, so the pilot dropped me off on the Binh Duc airfield where a security detachment met me and drove me back to Camp Viking.

*****

Within a brief period, the Viet Cong and North Vietnamese Army units attacked three of our units, separated by about eighty kilometers. Five men received serious wounds during the three events. One young engineer was paralyzed from the waist down and another was barely hanging on to life at the MASH in Dong Tam. The medics evacuated them to Japan in very critical condition. The three other engineers received lesser wounds. Despite the security measures we took, it was not possible to shield the men from every eventuality.

*****

Visits from Colonel Graves and Colonel Parfitt were less frequent during May. They seemed to be busy with the three construction battalions' projects. I did not miss the supervision from the higher echelons.

KIEN HOA PROVINCE

Toward the end of May the monsoon rains began to dampen the worksites. I was surprised to receive orders to rebuild some roads in Kien Hoa Province, which is across the Mekong River from My Tho. The province lies between two major branches of the Mekong River and at its widest point the province is about twenty-six kilometers. Those familiar with the lower Mississippi River Delta below New Orleans can understand the engineering challenge. The average elevation of the land is just above the river level and during the monsoon, when the Mekong rises, much of the province becomes inundated.

I flew to meet with the Vietnamese Province Chief and the Senior Province Advisor to coordinate the operation and learn about conditions in the area. Prior to that mission, there had been no US engineers in Kien Hoa Province. The Senior Advisor took me on a tour of the primary roads that seemed to be the most important for us to restore. That would be a big job for on company. My superiors and the staffs at Group and Brigade headquarters had no concept of the size and danger when they approved the mission.

Back at Camp Viking, I met with Bill Garcia to developed plans for the operation. All our companies were committed to projects, but Alpha Company was close to finishing its several missions. I decided to assign the mission to Lieutenant Rog's Alpha company. He worked with Bill to develop an operational plan for the work, the transport to Kien Hoa Province, supplies, and so on.

On 4 June a fleet of landing craft transported the men of Alpha Company, their vehicles, engineer equipment, ammunition, tents, fuel, food, and construction supplies across the Mekong River to their new base in Kien Hoa. Four CH-47 heavy lift helicopters supported the move. The move went surprisingly well, with no major problems. As soon as Alpha Company could set up a base camp, the men began working on the roads. I was dependent on CH-47 heavy lift helicopters and landing craft to supply Alpha Company.

*****

Naturally, there were problems. For example, a large equipment transporter truck and trailer, loaded with a D-7 bulldozer, drove onto an important bridge which collapsed under the load. The unit commander had not checked the bridge capacity; that is a basic responsibility for an engineer. Engineers should know better. It took two days and many resources to extract the equipment and rebuild the bridge.

*****

The US Province Senior Advisor for Long An Province was killed in action early in June. I met with the new Senior Advisor on 10 June to discuss the work that the 86th was performing in his province. Province Senior Advisors were Colonels who had been specially selected for the job. They had a tough job. Advising a foreign officer or civilian is very different from commanding US soldiers. I did not envy them. I had been an advisor in Vietnam in 1959-60 and found it very frustrating work.

NEW EXECUTIVE OFFICER

Major Giambruno completed a full year in Vietnam in June and the 34th Group Adjutant told me there were no majors available to assume the job. Once again, I was without a second in command and desperate to find an executive officer. I learned from Guy Jester that one of his officers, Major Bill Needham, was available. It seems that the 9th Division had plenty of engineer officers. I met Bill and at once accepted him as executive officer. Major Needham reported for duty on 11 June. I devoted the better part of a day to acquaint him with the operation of the battalion and the 34th Group. Needham was the battalion's third Executive Officer in ten months.

NEW OPERATIONS OFFICER

Bill Garcia also left the battalion in June. That was a joyful day for Bill, but a bad one for the battalion. Bill had served the battalion and his country above and beyond the call of duty. I am grateful to have served with Bill. More than any other officer, he was my right arm. The battalion could not have succeeded without him.

The best qualified officer in the battalion to serve as the Operations Officer was Captain Andy Dykes. Although Andy was a Captain, he had proven himself to be very capable; he had been a superb company commander. His Delta Company had been engaged in considerable combat operations and had carried out more combat engineering projects than any other company in the battalion.

There were other departures of men who were very important to our mission. Sergeant Major McCurley was evacuated to a hospital in Japan for surgery.

My faithful and courageous jeep driver, who never flinched from danger on our trips, left for home on emergency leave. His wife had suffered from a complete nervous breakdown worrying about him. It reminded me that the families back home were under great stress worrying about their sons and husbands.

*****

I could not believe the news when Colonel Graves told me that the USARV Inspector General was to inspect the battalion again. It was difficult for me to appreciate why another inspection would be of benefit to the battalion and the Army.

Figure 89 Thanking my jeep driver
as he leaves the battalion

TROOPS WITHDRAW

President Nixon met with President Thieu at Midway Island on 8 June and announced that he had ordered that 25,000 US troops to withdraw from Vietnam. A few days later, a "bombshell" landed at Camp Viking when Nixon's new Secretary of Defense, Melvin Laird, announced that the United States 9ᵗʰ Infantry Division would withdraw from Vietnam. That was the "beginning of the end." I could only guess that the Joint Chiefs of Staff thought that the situation in the Delta was so peaceful that the South Vietnamese could handle the war without the 9ᵗʰ Division.

News of the 9ᵗʰ Division's departure worried me. Without the 9ᵗʰ Division, my engineers would be more exposed to Viet Cong and North Vietnam Army attacks. Were my engineers to continue working on their projects without the division's support and security? With no artillery and chopper support from Dong Tam, the successful defense of Camp Viking from a major Viet Cong and North Vietnamese Army attack would be very risky.

The answer to my questions came on 20 June, U.S. Army Vietnam headquarters announced that the 86ᵗʰ Combat Engineer Battalion was to return to the United States for deactivation. Thus, the 86ᵗʰ was the first engineer battalion to withdraw from the war in Vietnam. The news spread rapidly among the men and they were excited to be going home early with the battalion. I had no information about the deactivation and was unable to answer my men's questions. Would all the men be going home? When would the battalion stop work on its assigned missions? Was our work in vain? What will we do with our weapons, vehicles, engineer equipment, and much else? What would happen to Camp Viking? There were more questions and I had no answers. Answers to those questions were slow to come because everyone, from the Pentagon down, was scrambling to put the President's orders into action.

I flew Long Binh to meet with Colonel Parfitt and the 20ᵗʰ Brigade staff on 22 June for instructions and learn some details so I could start planning for the stand-down and withdrawal of the battalion. There were hundreds of details to close out a battalion, but I flew back to Camp Viking with very few answers to my questions because Colonel Parfitt and his staff had not developed a plan. The next day I flew to Binh Thuy to meet with Colonel Graves and his staff, but they could not answer most of my questions. I was in the dark. Everyone seemed to be waiting for details from the Pentagon and U.S. Army Vietnam. I worked with the information I had, then made some assumptions about the unknown.

Colonel Graves did say that the battalion must continue work on our assigned missions. Our men were fighting the Viet Cong and the rain while working on jobs that they would abandon in a few weeks. My officers and men continued to execute their missions under very stressful conditions. However, I could see that the vigorous spirit of CAN DO was on the wane. The men lost all enthusiasm, and they were worried about their futures.

Finally, U.S. Army Vietnam announced that the men in the division and the battalion with more than two months left on their tour in Vietnam would be transferred to other units in Vietnam. Those with less than two months to serve in Vietnam would return to the United States. After the Adjutant sorted out that news he declared that 151 men would return to the US when the battalion left Vietnam. Understandably, most our men's morale dropped to an all-time low. It worried me, but I could do little to help them. They had developed friendships and cohesion within their squads, platoons, and companies and were upset because they were to transfer to other units as individual replacements destined for some unknown unit.

Yet, the war in the Delta was not over. So much for the peace plans in Paris and Washington. The battalion suffered more casualties after the 8 June meeting on Midway Island. The Viet Cong destroyed a major bridge east of My Tho and the battalion replaced that bridge with a one hundred forty-foot Bailey Bridge. On the night of 26 June, the Viet Cong fired several 107-mm rockets at the Tan An bridge and tried to sink the barge with the pile drive. One rocket hit the barge and tore a hole in the hull just above the water line. They missed the bridge. Our engineers welded a patch on the barge the next day. The roadwork in Kien Hoa Province was in terrible shape due to the intensity of the rains. I doubted if the engineers could complete the project under such wet conditions.

I flew back to Long Binh on 29 June to attend another meeting with Colonel Parfitt and all battalion and group commanders. It was an interesting session; however, when I realized that Colonel Parfitt and his staff was discussing plans for operations after the 86th was gone, I lost interest. I was tired and cared only about the future of the men in the 86th. There was no information about the deactivation of the 86th available at that meeting.

I received orders to transfer the 595 Light Equipment Company to the 35th Engineer Group, which was based at Cam Ranh Bay. The 595 Light Equipment Company was not an organic part of the 86th and was not on the list of units to return to the CONUS. The men of that company had performed magnificently. I withdrew the men and equipment from all construction projects and, on 30 June, I wished them well as they headed off for Cam Ranh Bay in a long convoy.

By the end of June, I believe that the enemy decided to reduce their attacks in our area and wait for the Americans in the Mekong Delta to leave. Why not, they won the battle in Paris and Washington. After the series of intensive attacks in June, there were just a few minor contacts. They knew they had won and were smart enough to lay low until the US units evacuated. They reduced their losses and built up their stocks for a push after we left. The ARVN would not be able to cope with a widespread attack across the Delta. I believed that the Viet Cong would own the Delta within a year, or less, after we left.

I was uncertain about my own future because my year in Vietnam would end late in July; however, I was not sure if I was to stay in country to deactivate the battalion. My answer arrived on 2 July. Orders directed that I report to the 90th Replacement Battalion at Camp Ling Binh on 14 July, for further assignment to the National War College in Washington D.C.

Several months earlier, Lieutenant Colonel Robert S. McGarry received orders to replace me at the end of my year in Vietnam. When the U.S. Army Vietnam decided that the battalion was to return to CONUS for deactivation, McGarry's orders were changed and he went on to command another battalion in Vietnam. However, Major Walter C. Bell arrived with orders to assume command of the battalion when I left. That would be a lousy assignment for Bell.

General Hollis invited me to a Fourth of July dinner in his Dong Tam mess. That evening was a total escape from the reality of the mud and the Viet Cong. Most of the division's battalion and brigade commanders were present as that may be the last time they would be together at Dong Tam. I knew many of them because the 86th was supporting them. At the end of the dinner, General Hollis made a short speech commending the 86th Engineers, and he noted my departure from the battalion. His comments were overly generous, and I appreciated them. I responded with a short "thank you" speech and told the other commanders how proud I was to have served with the 86th and to have supported the 9th Division. I flew back to Viking in a chopper with a

Long-Range Patrol that was going to land somewhere out in the Delta to gather more intelligence.

The ARVN Engineer at Can Tho presented the 86th Combat Engineer Battalion with two Republic of Vietnam awards, the Gallantry Cross with Palm for the period from January 1969 to July 1969 and the Civil Actions Honor Medal First Class for the period December 1968 to June 1969. That was a great honor for the battalion and well deserved, if I may say so. The award applied to every soldier in the battalion.

I conducted my last reconnaissance on 5 July because the 34th Group assigned a new mission for another road reconstruction project. It was hard to believe that staff officers at 20th Brigade and the 34th Group would send those orders. The mission needed a company and the use of amphibious landing craft to gain access to the area. The mission was absurd, so I told Colonel Graves that it would not be possible because the battalion's equipment and weapons were not available, and the men were busy processing their vehicles and engineer equipment for transfer to other units or to the depot.

I made my last visit to units of my battalion on 7 July. I thanked my company commanders for their great leadership and support and spoke to as many of my platoon leaders and platoon Sergeants that I could visit that day. I spent that night in Can Tho with my brother in-law, Joe Smith. It was my last chance to see him until he returned from Vietnam. I did not envy him working in the Delta after the 9th Division left.

I met with Colonel Graves and Brigadier General Kraft, Assistant Division Commander, on 8 July to clarify and coordinate details of the battalion's stand down. Some plans were beginning to take shape. The 93rd Construction Battalion was to take over some of our work. They transferred other missions to other engineer units. Orders directed that we clean and repair all vehicles and equipment before transferring them to other units or to depot storage. I tried to complete plans before my departure so that Major Bell could have a clear picture of his mission.

*****

At a simple ceremony at Camp Viking on 13 July 1969, Major Walter C. Bell assumed command of the 86th Combat Engineer Battalion. After the ceremony, I bade farewell to the fine officers and men that I had been honored to lead. For me it was over, but the war would continue.

I made my last helicopter ride when I flew from Camp Viking to the personnel-processing center in Long Binh where I joined the dehumanizing personnel processing system. I was angry again to see that they were handling enlisted combat veterans like cattle. Treatment for officers was slightly better. We discarded our Vietnam fatigues and donned khaki uniform and waited to get on a plane and never see Vietnam again in our lives. I was tired, but I was on my way home to be with my wife and my two wonderful children. The last paragraph of the last letter I wrote home before departing said, "I am weary - I am weary. This long day will soon be over."

Around 23:00 hours on 14 July 1969, I boarded a contract Boeing 707 along with a hundred or more Vietnam veterans. We sat quietly in our seats waiting for the big jet plane to move. There was a strange stillness in the cabin. As we taxied out to the runway, I thought of my first arrival in Vietnam in June 1959. Then the engines roared as the plane accelerated down the runway and then we felt the plane lift off. Still there was that strange silence. Finally, when we were airborne and out of small arms range, a tremendous cheer went up from the men. It was over, and we were going home to our loved ones in the United States.

My year with the 86th Engineer Combat Battalion was behind me. The battalion's achievements are of little note in the histories of the Vietnam War, but I shall never forget the officers and men that sacrificed so much for their country as the served in the 86th Combat Engineer Battalion.

SUMMARY

The men of the battalion had built important facilities for the base in Dong Tam, upgraded and constructed ten fire bases for the 9th Division, constructed or upgraded three important tactical airfields, cleared more than fifty thousand acres of jungle in the heart of the Mekong Delta, rebuilt and upgraded over one hundred miles of vital roads for military and civilian use, constructed many bridges of all types, protected a vital highway bridge, cleared thousands of mines and booby traps, built its own bases, and engaged in numerous combat operations with the 9th Division. The battalion's units worked at more than seventeen separate locations throughout the Delta region.

During the year the battalion suffered more than one hundred and fifty casualties. The leadership and valor of the men was recognized with the presentation of over five hundred awards of the Army Commendation Medal, The Bronze Star Medal, The Purple Heart, The Silver Star, and The Legion of Merit.

THE END

THE KEY PLAYERS
86th Combat Engineer Battalion

Battalion Headquarters

Commanding Officer	Lieutenant Colonel Ernest D. Peixotto
Commanding Officer	Major Walter C. Bell
Executive Officer	Major Paul C. Fleri, Jr.
Executive Officer	Major John T. Giambruno
Executive Officer	Major Needham
Adjutant	1st Lieutenant George A. Smigelski
Adjutant	Captain H. Rodney Nutt
S-2	Lieutenant DiGiacomo
S-2	Lieutenant Nickerson
S-2	1st Lt Felkner
S-2	1st Lt Michael R. Writt
S3	Major William Garcia
S-3	Captain Andy Dykes
Asst. S-3	1st Lt Yancey Jones
Asst. S-3	1st LT. Dennis Rog
Asst. S-3	1st Lieutenant Blewitt
S4	Captain Edwin C. Ajer
S-4	Captain F. T. Voorstadt,
Assistant S4	1st Lieutenant Dennis J. Rog
Property Book Officer	Chief Warrant Officer Clyde Kennedy
Maintenance Officer	1st Lieutenant Frank J. Schiralde
Maintenance Officer	Lt Walters
Asst. Maintenance Officer	Lieutenant Jeceski
Battalion Surgeon	Captain E. G. Vega
Battalion Surgeon	Captain Robert Falkner
Chaplain	Captain Harold C. Mills
Communications Officer	1st Lieutenant James Irvin
Communications NCO	Staff Sergeant Robert Thomas
Personnel Officer	CWO Stone
Battalion SGM	John E. Meeker
Battalion SGM	John McCurley

COMPANY OFFICERS
Lt Jezeski
Lt Langford

Headquarters Company
Company Commander	Captain Marion M. Meeks
Company Commander	1st. Lt. Lee Berglund
Company Commander	1st. Lt. James McLeod
Leader Heavy Equipment Sec	1st Lt Scott

Alpha Company
Company Commander	Captain Thomas Mouser
Company Commander	1st Lt. Dennis J. Rog
Executive Officer	1st Lt. William Brown
1st Platoon Leader	1st Lt. William C. Langford,
Platoon Leader	1st Lieutenant Felkner
1st Platoon Leader	Lieutenant Keroher
2nd Platoon Leader	Lt Bethke
3rd Platoon Leader	Lt Clay
First Sergeant	William E. Rose
First Sergeant	Clifford A. Edwards

Bravo Company
Company Commander	Captain Bernard W. Robinson
Company Commander	Name not revealed Relieved of command
Company Commander	Captain Richard H. Jones,
Executive Officer	1st Lt Albert Sorenson
Platoon Leader	1st Lt. Branin; FSB Danger
Platoon Leader	1st. Lt. Richard E. Kent
First Sergeant	1st Sgt. Lucion L. Cowart

Charlie Company
Company Commander	Captain Joseph M. Cidras
Company Commander	1st Lt. Stephen R. Bourke
Company Commander	1st Lt. Richard E. Kent
Company Commander	1st Lt. Harold F. Blewitt.
Executive Officer	1st Lt. William Brown
Executive Officer	1st Lt. Richard E. Kent
Platoon Leader	1st Lt. Speed

Delta Company

Company Commander	Captain Joseph G. Huber, April '86 to
Company Commander	Captain Andy Dykes, June 21, 1968
Company Commander	1st Lt. Larry Warden, 29 May from Dykes
Company Commander	1st Lt. Joseph L. Paveza, 6 July
Executive Officer	1st Lieutenant Incerti
Platoon Leader	1st Lieutenant Joseph C. Paveza
First Sergeant	1st Sgt. Waite
Motor Sergeant	Lawrence J. Bryant

595 Engineer Company (Light Equipment)

Company Commander	Captain Charles W. Zang, to 30 Sept
Company Commander	1st Lt. Yancey Jones, 30 Sept
Company Commander	Captain Albert A. Sorenson, in April
Support Platoon Leader	1st Lt. Bourke
2nd Platoon Leader	1st Lieutenant Stephen N. Dettor
Platoon Leader	Lieutenant Timothy M. Peterson

Delta Company, 168 Engineer Battalion

Company Commander	Captain Antonio Janarro
Platoon Leader	1st Lt Michael Shelton
Platoon Leader	1st Lt Ellis Bassetti
Platoon Leader	1st Lt John Bendure
First Sergeant	1st SSgt Herbert L. Teague

20th Brigade

Commanding Officer	MG Curtis W. Chapman
Commanding Officer	Colonel (P) Harold R. Parfitt
Deputy Commanding Officer	Colonel Victor O. Wilson

34th Group

Commanding Officer	Colonel William Stewart
Commanding Officer	Colonel Ernest Graves, Jr.
Executive Officer	Lieutenant Colonel Clyde Lawrence

CPSIA information can be obtained
at www.ICGtesting.com
Printed in the USA
BVHW08s1520290818
525940BV00005B/190/P